DAVID BECKHAM

FIFTY DEFINING FIXTURES

Steve Tongue

AMBERLEY

First published 2015

Amberley Publishing
The Hill, Stroud
Gloucestershire, GL5 4EP

www.amberley-books.com

British Library Cataloguing in Publication Data.
A catalogue record for this book is available from the British Library.

ISBN 978 1 4456 4641 1 (print)
ISBN 978 1 4456 4642 8 (ebook)

Typesetting and Origination by Amberley Publishing.
Printed in the UK.

Contents

Foreword

When I started working with David Beckham at Manchester United in 1999 what I found was a model professional, and he was still the same when I brought him back into the England team some eight years later: low-maintenance, the hardest of workers, always wanting to improve. There was no one better in that respect.

David was one of what I call sport's 5 per centers, who reach the top of their profession not just through ability but with tremendous determination and mental strength. It can sometimes mean living on the edge. As this book recalls, David had a bad time when he was sent off at the World Cup in 1998, and he could have gone under. Instead, he used that as part of his development and, helped by the support of his club, he became better than ever.

The following year United completed the Treble in that amazing finish against Bayern Munich following two Beckham corner-kicks. And don't think that was just luck, any more than the famous goal he struck from another set piece for England against Greece, taking us to the 2002 World Cup finals.

It was a skill honed through practice from a young age, day after day, year after year. I've never seen anything like the attention to detail as he practised those free-kicks. It became a trademark and one that won his team many games.

When I became manager of England in 2006, David had just resigned the captaincy and my thinking was that we needed a new start, so I left him out of the squad. Things didn't go quite as well as we hoped and within a few months we came to think his sheer presence was needed. He was more than happy, as he always was and always will be, to help his country out, and bringing him back was one of the best things that could have happened to the team.

Then there is David Beckham the person. At a team hotel, with dozens of people outside, most of the players would walk straight through; he would stand there and sign every autograph, not for show or image, but because he is such a genuinely nice guy.

I was proud to have worked with him for club and country and hope you enjoy reliving the matches in these pages.

Steve McClaren

Introduction

'Ah, Beckham! I think he is more famous than me, definitely!'

Nelson Mandela.

'The most overrated footballer in the history of the game.'

James Lawton in *The Independent*.

'It's a bit like *The Truman Show*. I'm not complaining because it is a huge privilege to be famous. But it can be surreal.'

David Beckham.

Googling 'David Beckham' produces over 100 million references. Facebook likes are running at over 50 million and rising. In the United States, where 'soccer' is a minor sport, he once stood at number five on *Forbes* 'most powerful celebrities' list – just behind Beyonce and comfortably ahead of his friend Brad Pitt.

When he was injured before one World Cup, the matter was discussed at cabinet level. When it happened again, eight years later, the Poet Laureate produced an ode in his honour. Leading filmmaker Sam Taylor-Johnson made a video of him sleeping. The eminent social historian and Aldershot fan, Professor David Kynaston, has spoken of the 'Beckhamisation' of football, as though David himself is personally responsible for the overblown state of the game.

Retiring as a professional footballer in 2013 hardly diminished his profile. Since 1 January 2014 I have been receiving a daily email, listing every mention of him in British newspapers; there has not yet been a single blank day, whether he is making what passes for news in today's celebrity culture, or simply acting as a reference point, cultural or sporting.

This book, independent rather than officially authorised, aims to follow a thread through the long-running Beckham Show, while keeping the most important thing – the football – at its heart. 'Overrated' as my former colleague Jim Lawton believed, or not, he became an integral part of the Manchester United side that grew out of the fabled 'Class of 92' to dominate English football during his twelve years at Old Trafford. He had a hand – or a foot – in some of the defining goals of the period, and with 115 international appearances was one of the so-called golden generation supposed to carry the national team to glory for the first time since 1966.

I happened to be at the match at Brighton in September 1992, working on the BBC radio commentary of the game, when a seventeen-year-old Beckham first realised his dream. It was an obsession shared with millions of boys all over the world, but in this case was brought to fruition by a combination of natural ability and hard work. Even Beckham's greatest critics have never denied him the latter quality. If many are called, or want to be, few are chosen (especially by Manchester United and Real Madrid). Once they are, then in the modern world of celebrity magazines and tabloid wars, paparazzi and social media, a Cristiano Ronaldo or David Beckham are considered fair game and can come to feel their life is as public as Truman's in Peter Weir's film – on show twenty-four hours a day all over the globe.

But, to reiterate, the focus here is on Beckham the footballer and the most memorable or significant of his 800-plus matches. As other authors in this series have pointed out, selecting fifty games is not easy and cannot be definitive. The choice made in these pages reflects every period of a career in five countries, during which Beckham, a player of supposedly limited talent, became the first Englishman to win league titles in four different ones, including England and Spain.

The most obvious games are here including, of course, the spectacular goal from the halfway line at Wimbledon in 1996 where Beckham says 'the madness' really began, his often forgotten contribution to the unforgettable conclusion of United's European Cup win of 1999, the infamous red card against Argentina and subsequent redemption after pulling England's crucial World Cup qualification game against Greece out of the Old Trafford fire almost single handed, winning over first Madrid's Bernabeu after a difficult start, and later the Home Depot Center – a wonderfully named stadium in such a glamorous city as Los Angeles – in similar circumstances.

Early chapters switch between Manchester United during the stunningly successful nineties period and a flowering England career before the growing strain on relations with Sir Alex Ferguson: the infamous injury the manager inflicts on Beckham with a stray boot and the final rupture. For later games the venues encompass Spain, South Africa (for a tearful resignation in a marquee after failing to end English football's forty-four years of hurt) Los Angeles and Paris.

After deciding to make the move to the US – and being derided for doing so – Beckham is dropped by Madrid's manager Fabio Capello, but typically shows such determination that the Italian martinet is forced to reinstate him, and Real are rewarded with a Spanish League title at last. Here is a theme for the last half-dozen years of an astonishing career: criticised, even written off, in first Madrid, then Los Angeles ('go home fraud' one placard said), he grits his teeth, relies as ever on the old maxim that the more you practise the luckier you get, and proves more than a few people wrong. Having done so, he hangs up his personalised boots to a further round of contrasting reviews, ending a story that can happily be told through the medium that matters most – on the football pitch.

Steve Tongue,
London, 2015.

Manchester United Under-16s 4 Liverpool 1
Milk Cup Quarter-Final
(Portstewart, Co. Derry)
25 July 1991

The Beckhams may, for a while, have been a family divided in terms of football allegiance, but for David Robert Joseph, born in a Leytonstone hospital in May 1975, there was really only ever one club. The name Joseph came from his grandfather Joe, a print worker and Tottenham Hotspur supporter, but father Ted's allegiance to Manchester United, stemming like many of his generation from the 1958 Munich air disaster, proved the stronger influence.

A video exists of David, aged three, wearing United kit bought by dad for Christmas, and although Joe, who countered by regularly buying Spurs shirts, was delighted that his grandson trained for a while at Tottenham, that was only because United were not yet allowed to approach boys from outside their area. Even then he wore a red shirt and was worried only that he would not cross the Manchester club's radar.

He did so in 1986, firstly when watched by a scout playing for Waltham Forest schools and then by winning a prize from the Bobby Charlton Soccer Schools, which involved performing on the Old Trafford pitch, ironically before a game against Spurs – visiting fans initially cheered when hearing he was from London, then booed when he was described as a United supporter.

Despite being offered a six-year deal by Tottenham from the age of twelve, he and his father knew United were hooked. Plain Alex Ferguson had caused great excitement by ringing their Chingford home, inviting David to be a mascot for a League game at West Ham, where he sat next to the manager on the bench, and on his thirteenth birthday in May 1988, the 'happiest day of my life', he signed an identical deal to Tottenham's at Old Trafford.

The *Rothmans Yearbook* of 1990–91 contains his first entry, in (very) small print on the list of Manchester United players as 'Associated Schoolboys', together with 'Butt, Nicholas', 'Neville, Gary' and 'Scholes, Paul' among others. By the following year's edition that had become 'Associated Schoolboys who have accepted the club's offer of a Traineeship/Contract', and the Class of '92 was taking shape.

Ted and Sandra Beckham were the most supportive of parents, often acting as bad cop/good cop when dad's demands of his son in practice and training, however well intentioned, became excessive. In the summer of 1991 they made a first trip out of England to watch him when United took part in the Milk Cup competition in Northern Ireland – an annual invitation event for foreign as well as British youth teams.

Nobby Stiles, World Cup winner and United hero, was the youth team coach, and in an important show of faith he had made Beckham captain. The team would go on to win the tournament, but it was the quarter-final victory over Liverpool that gave them as much pleasure as anything.

At senior level, United were only just beginning to emerge from Liverpool's shadow after five years under Ferguson, and although Manchester City and Leeds United, both of whom finished above them that year, were serious and unloved foes, it was clearly understood at all levels of the club that the rivalry with Liverpool was something special.

Beckham had already experienced Anfield when turning out for Essex Schoolboys the previous season in an Inter-County Cup final there against a Merseyside team including Robbie Fowler. Now Fowler was in opposition again, against a United side in which Stiles was clearly right to have every confidence. Although the boys were regularly warned that only 1 per cent of youth team players would ever make the first team, no fewer than six of United's would eventually do so, as well as Paul Scholes, who was one of the substitutes, while Robbie Savage and Colin Murdock went on to become full internationals with other clubs.

Manchester United: Pollock, G. Neville, O'Kane, Murdock, Riley, Beckham, Butt, Roberts, Gillespie, Savage, Thornley.
Liverpool : Embleton, Jones, Stalker, Neal, Brydon, Nestor, Whittaker, Scott, Fowler, McAvee, Charnock.

United had won their group by beating Ballymena United 1-0 and Akureyri of Iceland 9-1 (with a hat-trick by Butt), then drawing 1-1 with Hearts. In the best traditions of the rivalry between United and Liverpool, both of whom have always had huge followings on either side of the Irish border, there was then a heated row before the quarter-final game because Stiles and the Liverpool staff, headed by Steve Heighway, both insisted on wearing red shirts.

Stiles found a way out of the deadlock when United were offered green ones, and he cannily foresaw an increase in neutral support if his lads wore Northern Ireland colours with their usual black socks.

The result, Stiles recalls, was 'a slaughter', even if his autobiography exaggerates the final score as 5-1. United had exciting wingers in Keith Gillespie on the right, who scored a hat-trick, and Ben Thornley on the left, who was voted player of the tournament and would have had a much better career had injuries not hampered him at an early age. Beckham, running the game from central midfield, took the captain's responsibility in converting a penalty for the other goal.

In the semi-final against Motherwell, he incurred the manager's displeasure and then admiration. First he missed a penalty, and with the goalless game going into extra-time was shunted out to the right to bring Scholes into the centre. According to Stiles' recollection,

> Beckham put on a massive sulk. It was infuriating to see such a talented player letting himself down like that, but when extra-time was over and we still had to go to penalties, I saw something in him that I liked very much and almost made me forget what had gone before.

What he meant was that self-belief, despite having played below his best, encouraged Beckham to grab the ball for United's second penalty of the shoot-out and smash it into the net. They went through 5-3 on penalties and in the final beat Hearts 2-0 with goals by Thornley and Savage.

Still at that stage the Class of '91, United's new babes under captain Beckham were up and running.

Crystal Palace Under-18s 1
Manchester United 3
FA Youth Cup Final First Leg (Selhurst Park)
14 April 1992

It was clear to everyone involved that Manchester United had found a special group of young players. If the core were local lads, from places like Bury and Oldham, Ferguson's insistence on improving the scouting network throughout Britain, and the pulling power of United's name, meant that others were recruited from far and wide. Winger Keith Gillespie arrived from Northern Ireland, Robbie Savage, a centre forward at the time, from Wales and from East London came a kid called Beckham.

Having been together longest, the locals like Gary Neville, Nicky Butt, Paul Scholes, Chris Casper, Ben Thornley and Ryan Giggs (whose family moved from Wales to Salford when he was six) might have resented the incomers. 'Flash' was Neville's first impression of both Savage and Beckham – whom he recalls as rather skinny with gelled hair, and, worst of all, a Cockney.

Yet the youth team dressing room was nothing if not meritocratic. What mattered was ability, ambition, a capacity for work and preferably the sort of love for the Reds that Neville saw in the young London recruit.

For any junior side, however well they may do in their regional league, the most exciting test is the FA Youth Cup – a competition that mattered more to Manchester United than any other club. Like Real Madrid with the European Cup, United had dominated the early years of the tournament in the fifties, winning the first five finals.

There was another success in 1964, but thereafter only a couple of losing finals, including a painful one in 1986 against local rivals Manchester City, who Ferguson believed were somehow sweeping up the best local talent at the time.

By the 1991–92 season, however, it was clear that United would have a chance again even though a majority of the team were first-year apprentices rather than second-years like Giggs – already a regular in the first team but playing as captain for the Youth Cup games when possible. Beckham became established in midfield with Butt during a run that started in the second round with a 4-2 win at Sunderland. Walsall were beaten 2-1, City joyfully dismissed 3-1 away from home, then Tranmere were beaten 2-0 in the quarter-final.

The semi-finals were over two legs and United beat a promising Tottenham team in both games, 3-0 and 2-1, to set up a final against Crystal Palace, who had narrowly beaten their Selhurst Park tenants Wimbledon and were given home advantage for the first leg.

Crystal Palace: Glass, Clark, Cutler, Holman, Edwards, McPherson (Sparrow, 32), Hawthorne, Rollison, Thompson (McCall, 77), Watts, Ndah.
Manchester United: Pilkington, Switzer, Neville, Casper, O'Kane, Davies, Beckham, Butt, Thornley, McKee, Savage (Roberts, 82).
Attendance: 7,825.

To the team's disappointment, Giggs was not available for the away leg, as United's seniors, duelling with Leeds United at the top of the First Division, were about to embark on a tortuous programme of five games in eleven days, of which he would start every one. (They won only the first and were denied a first League title in twenty-five years by four points).

Giggs was just as disappointed himself, although he has admitted finding the Youth Cup games even more stressful than first-team matches:

I found it more taxing to play in those games alongside my mates than I did to face the likes of Leeds and Liverpool as a regular member of the first team. Maybe it was because everybody was straining every sinew to prove themselves, to make the big breakthrough.

Giggs felt Butt was the squad's outstanding player, while Scholes, 'although there was never any doubt about his ability', was considered at that point too small, which was why he missed the final.

The Palace side, although workmanlike, significantly contained barely one player whose name would be widely recognised today in striker George Ndah, for whom Wolverhampton Wanderers would eventually play Palace £1 million, plus, perhaps, goalkeeper Jimmy Glass, who would become a Carlisle United legend seventeen years later by scoring the goal that kept them in the Football League.

After a day of rain in London, there was some doubt about whether the Selhurst pitch would be playable, but a heavy surface proved no deterrent to United's youngsters or to Beckham, who scored a crucial goal. Unusually it came from his left foot, hammered in on the volley from the edge of the penalty area to delight his watching father, who must have reflected on the value of all those days on Chingford fields, impressing on David the importance of being able to strike the ball with both feet. It was a spectacular effort, although he would better it with a more famous one on the same ground four years later (see Chapter 12).

After 17 minutes, Glass failed to hold a shot by Butt from a cross by Ben Thornley, who was generally agreed to be man of the match. Thornley's interception of a backpass then set up Beckham for the second, and although Palace substitute Stuart McCall (not the future Scottish international and Rangers manager) retrieved one goal near the end, there was still time for Beckham to cross for Butt to score his second, paving the way for the club's first Youth Cup success in almost thirty years, since George Best's team of 1964.

'The visitors confirmed their pre-match billing as favourites and demonstrated their ominous strength in depth,' reported *The Daily Telegraph*.

Not that formidable coach Eric Harrison, who would occasionally bawl out Beckham for trying what he called 'Hollywood passes', would allow any complacency in the tiresome wait of over a month before the second leg. The one advantage of waiting so long was that the League season was over and Giggs could lead the team at Old Trafford, where 14,681 turned out to see a 3-2 victory for a comfortable aggregate success of 6-3.

David Meek, United correspondent for the *Manchester Evening News* since 1958, commended 'terrific teamwork studded with magical creative play'. Ferguson praised Brian Kidd for his recruitment work, pointing out that seven of the starting XI hailed from Greater Manchester or Lancashire, and Palace's manager Steve Coppell, a former Old Trafford hero, said, 'It's clear that the conveyor belt producing young players is moving again'.

The following season, with Beckham's year still available, United reached the final again only to lose both legs to Leeds 2-0 at Old Trafford, and after another month's wait, 2-1 at Elland Road. The attendance figures were remarkable: 30,562 and 31,037, respectively.

Although upset at the time, Beckham came to see that defeat as the sort of setback to make a young player of the right mentality stronger, reflecting, 'For most of us it was the first big disappointment of our footballing lives and perhaps it made us stronger, having to experience it together. You want to make sure you don't feel that down again in the future.'

As with the beaten Crystal Palace team, few of the Leeds side would become first-team players, emphasising how hard it was to make the jump and what an extraordinary crop United had brought together.

Brighton 1 Manchester United 1
Coca-Cola Cup Second Round, First Leg
(Goldstone Ground)
23 September 1992

Early on in the 1992–93 season, the seventeen-year-old Beckham began training with the seniors, and on 16 September he was an unused substitute for the UEFA Cup tie at home to Torpedo Moscow. Only 19,998 were present at Old Trafford, where building work was going on, and in a disappointing goalless draw Gary Neville beat him into the first team by coming on for the last few minutes. But Beckham's own chance was to come a week later.

United were the League Cup holders, having beaten Nottingham Forest 1-0 at Wembley in April, registering a trophy for the third successive year to follow the 1990 FA Cup and then the European Cup-Winners Cup. Ferguson was on a roll, having been allowed three-and-a-half years since replacing Ron Atkinson to secure his first trophy and finally winning over most critics by adding two more, although finishing positions in the League remained erratic: 11th, 2nd, 11th, 13th, 6th and 2nd.

It would be another two years before he introduced the concept of resting several players for the League Cup (see Chapter 6), and for the opening match in defence of the trophy United always intended to put out a near full-strength side, making an exception only for Giggs, who the manager was concerned about overusing and wanted to keep for the second leg against Torpedo. Several of the Class of '92 were taken along for the ride, which proved to be an uncomfortable flight to the South Coast in a seventeen-seater plane, although none of them were listed in the squad of thirteen given to that day's *Manchester Evening News*.

United's party stayed at the Grand Hotel, (bombed by the IRA at the Conservative Party conference eight years earlier), and although Ted and Sandra Beckham had travelled down, their son was hardly expecting to be included, not least because forty-eight hours earlier he had played in a rather less glamorous fixture away to Rotherham United reserves. Ferguson left it until inside the dressing room an hour before the game before announcing the team, whereupon Ben Thornley rushed out to see Beckham's parents, shouting 'David's on the bench!'

Brighton: Beeney, Chivers, Foster, McCarthy, Chapman, Crumplin, Codner, Wilkins, Walker, Kennedy, Edwards.
Manchester United: Walsh, Irwin, Bruce, Pallister, Martin, Kanchelskis (Beckham, 72), Webb, Ince, Wallace, Hughes, McClair.
Attendance: 16,649.

Brighton, United's dogged opponents from the 1983 FA Cup final, were a workmanlike side from the top half of the old Second Division, but they fell behind to a fine goal by Danny Wallace, curling the ball high into the net from 20 yards.

Eighteen minutes from the end came the moment the Beckham family had been waiting for: David was sent on for his first-team debut in place of the flying Ukrainian winger Andrei Kanchelskis. He was so excited, he banged his head on the dug-out roof, while up in the main stand Ted was shaking. 'It was all I'd ever dreamed about, seeing my son in a Manchester United shirt.'

What the proud parents might not have noted was brought to the attention of *Manchester Evening News* readers the next day: 'While the youngster was delivering instructions to reorganise the team, his opposing full-back raided forward. Ian Chapman's swinging centre was headed in at the far post by Edwards.'

The *MEN* report did note, however, that Wallace almost scored again from a Beckham pass, and awarded the teenager a respectable mark of 7/10, with only Gary Walsh, Paul Ince and man of the match Wallace receiving anything higher. Ferguson, as well as keeping the young man's feet on the ground with a mild ticking off, was not happy, complaining, 'We didn't get motivated. We treated it like a practise match and we almost lost it near the end.'

The *Daily Mail* praised the home side's comeback, noting,

> Brighton displayed tremendous commitment, evoking memories of their 1983 FA Cup
> final against United, and had the better of the chances. But a combination of goalkeeper
> Gary Walsh's ability, and careless finishing frustrated them.

Ferguson would have more to grumble about the following week when United suffered a second goalless draw against Torpedo and went out of the UEFA Cup on penalties. In the second leg of the League Cup they struggled past Brighton 1-0 with a goal by Mark Hughes before going out at Aston Villa in the third round and ending the hopes of further involvement that season for the Beckham generation.

The consolation for David came in January, completing his apprenticeship and signing a first professional contract on £200 a week, with a handsome £30,000 signing-on fee. Two months later, United's youngsters were given the task of analysing their performances in writing and in mock television interviews. Ferguson, according to one observer, smiled as Beckham shared his dream: 'I hope to play for United's first team in the next couple of years and emulate my hero, Bryan Robson.'

Port Vale 1 Manchester United 2
Coca-Cola Cup Second Round, First Leg (Vale Park) 21 September 1994

As Manchester United finally achieved a long-awaited League title in May 1993 – now known as the Premiership – and added the club's first League and FA Cup double the following season, there was little scope for further promotion of the young bloods. 'Rotation' was yet to become a buzzword.

In 1992–93, seven United players appeared in forty or more of the forty-two League games, and the following season five of them did the same, with eight more appearing at least thirty times. There was essentially a first-choice squad of thirteen or fourteen players, of whom Giggs and the slightly older Lee Sharpe were the only representatives of the new generation.

In the first Championship season, Nicky Butt's one game as a substitute was the only League appearance by any of the latter group, highly regarded as they were. The following campaign Butt again came on just once. Ben Thornley did the same and in the final game, with a second title already won and the Cup Final looming, Gary Neville and Colin McKee were given a League debut.

So two years on from the Brighton game, Beckham had still not played again for the first team, having had to settle for being part of United's reserve team which won the Central League in 1994 for the first time in sixteen years. Now his chance came again, this time in tandem with so many contemporaries that questions would be asked about the team selection at Parliament.

The League Cup, although its name was forever changing (and still is), was very much a first-team competition. Premiership managers filling the side with reserves was unheard of until Ferguson broke the mould one Wednesday night in the Potteries. His reasoning was not just that his babes needed the opportunity, but that the Champions League had expanded, with a group stage now introduced before Christmas. United were guaranteed a minimum of six games in it and the League Cup cropped up in between the first two of them – at home to IFK Gothenburg and away to Galatasaray.

To widespread consternation, the manager therefore named a side showing an unprecedented nine changes from the one that had beaten Liverpool four days earlier. Only David May and Denis Irwin kept their place as Ferguson brought in five nineteen-year-olds, as well as, it should be said, the returning Roy Keane and Brian McClair.

Port Vale: Musselwhite, Sandeman, Griffiths, D Glover, Tankard, Kent, Porter, Van der Laan, L Glover, Foyle, Naylor (Burke, 70).
Manchester United: Walsh, G Neville (O'Kane, 77), May, Keane, Irwin, Gillespie, Beckham, Butt (Sharpe, 82), Davies, McClair, Scholes.
Attendance: 18,605.

Newly promoted Port Vale were only one division below United and had made a good start to the season, fifth place that September being just about the highest point in their history. When Lee Glover scored for them in the seventh minute, knives were being sharpened for Ferguson, but they soon had to be sheathed.

The equaliser came shortly before the interval when Scholes latched onto a backpass and shot in off the post. In the fifty-fourth minute he added what proved to be the winner, ducking onto a cross by the twenty-year-old Simon Davies to head past Paul Musselwhite. Scholes therefore earned the headlines, including those in *The Independent,* where Phil Shaw wrote,

On the day Gary Lineker announced his retirement, another teenager added his name to the burgeoning list of strikers vying to inherit his mantle in the late Nineties. Paul Scholes, a contemporary of Robbie Fowler and Noel Whelan in the England Youth side, marked his Manchester United debut with two nonchalantly taken goals at Vale Park last night.

Against bigger, stronger opponents ... Alex Ferguson's fledglings might have been expected to cave in. Instead, they allied superior touch and mobility to surprising maturity, and Vale's embarrassment was compounded by a gloating chorus of '2-1 to the Youth Team' from the visitors' end. It was men against boys – but this time the boys were in a different class.

That was not sufficient to impress the local MP, Joan Walley, who complained to the Football League and the All Party Parliamentary Football Group that Vale's unusually large crowd had bought their tickets in expectation of seeing Eric Cantona, Mark Hughes, Ryan Giggs, Peter Schmeichel and the rest.

Fans writing to the local paper took up the theme, with one suggesting 'We were all conned into parting with our money,' and another adding, 'If I pay to see Frank Sinatra, I don't expect to see Rolf Harris!'

For Beckham and his young mates, however, it was all further valuable experience against seasoned Second Division opposition not prepared to allow them any liberties. They would face another challenge in the next round, as Ferguson made clear after the match, telling reporters,

I'll be doing this throughout the Coca-Cola Cup. With Europe next week and internationals coming, most people expect me to do the sensible thing. It may incur the wrath of the League, I don't know, but we'll be doing what's right for Manchester United. The inexperience helped us out there. They didn't have a care and played without fear. It must have been hard for Port Vale facing that.

He lived up to his promise, fielding a similar side for the third round, even though it was away to Premiership leaders Newcastle United. Kevin Keegan's team, close to full strength, won with late goals by Philippe Albert and Paul Kitson, but Ferguson recalled of the new generation in his autobiography: '[They were] ... absolutely brilliant, only losing out in the last ten minutes because of fatigue. It was clear now that I had youngsters equipped to play at the highest level.'

For David Beckham, that would soon mean the Champions League.

Manchester United 4 Galatasaray 0
Champions League (Old Trafford)
7 December 1994

Because of UEFA's complicated rules on eligibility, picking teams for European games was a problem for English clubs. Only five foreign players were allowed, the catch being that 'foreign' included all Scottish, Welsh and Irish players unless they had come through a club's youth system.

With Peter Schmeichel, Andrei Kanchelskis and the talismanic Eric Cantona (signed in November 1992) among the growing contingent of European players in English football, Alex Ferguson had to juggle a squad whose first-choice starting XI would not have been allowed.

The European Cup, however it was now renamed, was a competition of huge significance to the club and there was bitter disappointment that their return to it in 1993–94, after an absence of twenty-five years, lasted only two rounds; Galatasaray of Turkey forced a 3-3 draw at Old Trafford and held on amid wild scenes on and off the pitch in Istanbul for a 0-0 draw to go through on away goals.

Drawn together in the same group the following year, the teams again played out a goalless draw in Turkey, which together with a home win over IFK Gothenburg and a draw at home to Barcelona (which Ferguson felt should have been a victory), seemed to put United in reasonable shape at halfway.

The UEFA regulations did offer opportunities for the younger generation of Englishmen. Beckham, Scholes and Gary Neville were all unused substitutes for the Gothenburg game, and Nicky Butt, regarded by many as the best of the bunch at that time, started the first four group matches. If the opening three had been satisfactory, however, the fourth brought a 4-0 defeat in Barcelona, with Beckham again on the bench, and the manager was criticised for leaving out Schmeichel in order to play an extra non-Englishman. Ferguson insists to this day that goalkeeper Gary Walsh was not to blame for any of the goals, but the result, when followed by an avoidable 3-1 defeat away to Gothenburg, meant United were on the verge of elimination.

To qualify, they had to beat Galatasaray and hope that the Swedes, who topped the group, went to Barcelona and won. The second part of that equation always looked the trickier one, and in *The Daily Telegraph* preview, Henry Winter suggested, 'Everyone agrees that even Red Adair would struggle to rescue Red hopes of staying in the Champions Cup.'

After studying several European games from his place in the dug-out, Beckham had been encouraged to believe he might start this time by a report in the *Manchester Evening News* suggesting there would be a chance for some of the youngsters – and so it proved. Seven first-teamers were unavailable through ineligibility or suspension and Ferguson, confident of beating the Turks for the first time in four meetings, picked teenagers Gary Neville, Butt and Beckham, plus Simon Davies, age twenty, to start the game, telling reporters the day beforehand, 'The younger players won't be afraid. They will run their socks off.'

> **Manchester United:** Walsh, G Neville, Bruce, Pallister, Irwin, Beckham, Keane, Butt, Davies, Cantona, McClair.
> **Galatasaray:** Stauce, Sedat, Bulent, Maert, Suat, Tugay (Yusuf, 63), Hamza (Ugar, 46),Ergun, Arif, Turkyilmaz, Hakan.
> **Attendance:** 39,220.

One milestone for Beckham, a first European appearance, became a second one half-an-hour into the game. As *The Telegraph* reported the next day, 'Pressure from Eric Cantona and Brian McClair, influential older heads in such an inexperienced side, forced Bulent to clear but only to Beckham, whose low drive from the edge of the penalty area comfortably beat Stauce.'

Comfortable or not, he admitted later it was something of a mishit, but the young Manchester United fanatic had achieved another dream, scoring for the first team, and at the Stretford End too. And who was this, grabbing him in celebration?

> Eric Cantona was the first player to get to me. I was buzzing that much, he was having to fight me off in the end. I just wouldn't let go of him. We played well and the fact that there were so many of the younger boys in the team made it even better. Starting the game had made a difference too. I felt a lot more at home at Old Trafford that night than I had during my seventeen minutes down at Brighton.

To further the cause of the young generation, Davies had scored in the first couple of minutes following a run and cross from the right by Neville. Keane added a third goal in the second half after good link-up play between Beckham and Cantona, and an own goal by Bulent meant an emphatic victory. As expected, Barcelona avoided defeat at home to Gothenburg, which meant that those two went into the quarter finals (where both were beaten). *The Telegraph* summed it up:

> Bravely, at times brilliantly, Manchester United won the battle; dispiritingly, they lost the war. A dashing defeat of Galatasaray at Old Trafford last night was not enough. The fatal damage to United's European Cup aspirations had been inflicted by the other, infamous 4-0 scoreline at the Nou Camp last month.

Reports praised the youngsters in particular, Ferguson adding, 'I was proud of them tonight. That was the way to do it, just go out and enjoy yourself.'

Beckham had proved he could live in and against exalted company, even if an element of hero worship remained in his attitude to Cantona. He was therefore as shocked as anyone, when sitting in the stand at Selhurst Park one night in the month after the Galatasaray game to see the Frenchman commit his astonishing assault on an abusive Crystal Palace supporter after being sent off for the fifth time in United colours.

Beckham's autobiography, while admitting he was 'not saying what he did was right', is exceptionally sympathetic about the incident – a view coloured perhaps by the highly personal abuse he suffered at later stages of his own career.

United banned Cantona for the rest of the season, hoping to forestall further Football Association action, and were dismayed when the FA added a further four months, ruling him out until the following September. Although United had signed Andy Cole from Newcastle just beforehand for a significant sum, Cantona's absence seriously affected their chances of success in the two remaining competitions that season – the Premiership (they were lying second at the time) and the FA Cup. They would eventually win nothing.

In the latter, a home draw against Wrexham offered Beckham his debut in the competition as a substitute for McClair during a 5-2 win, when an even younger Phil Neville made his debut. There were further games too for his older brother Gary, and Butt, Scholes and John O'Kane in the early rounds.

For the fifth round against old rivals Leeds, Ferguson reverted to his strongest side, and by the time of the quarter-final in March, Beckham, to his surprise, would be playing elsewhere.

Preston North End 2 Doncaster Rovers 2
Division Three (Deepdale)
4 March 1995

Called into Alex Ferguson's office at the end of February 1995 and told that a bottom-division club wanted him on loan, David Beckham's first reaction was panic. Was this how little United thought of him?

While the young guns were all pleased to see their contemporaries progressing, there was inevitably a certain envy too of those going fastest. Beckham had noted how Scholes and the feistier Butt were now regular substitutes for the first team: before the turn of the year Gary Neville had appeared in nine successive League games; Davies and Gillespie, both wide players like David, had started three games apiece before Gillespie moved to Newcastle as part of the Andy Cole transfer; and that month even Phil Neville, eighteen months younger than Beckham, had beaten him to a League debut, in the Manchester derby as well.

No wonder he quickly sought reassurance from his father and the reserve team coach Eric Harrison, after which Ferguson had him back in the office to spell out United's thinking more clearly: the move was designed purely to get him some regular games and toughen him up.

Proud Preston, as the club liked to be known, had been founder members and first-ever winners of the Football League, completing that inaugural season unbeaten and adding the FA Cup – Double winners 105 years before Manchester United managed it. By 1995 they were in the old Fourth Division, now restyled as the Endsleigh Football League Division Three, sitting just outside the play-off places and needing a push for the remaining two months of the season. This was football at the coalface, undertaken by players who knew that the next stop down was the dole.

The manager was Gary Peters, a Londoner who had played for Reading, Fulham and Wimbledon; the centre half and captain was a Glaswegian called David Moyes.

Beckham, while reassured by Ferguson's lecture, was understandably nervous. At United, inexperienced or not, he was part of a clearly promising young group of great potential. At Deepdale he was walking into a dressing room full of old salts, whose thoughts he imagined as 'here's this big time Charlie from United and a Cockney as well'.

Then there was the culture shock of facilities at a far lower level, throwing his kit on the floor after the first training session and before taking a shower brought an immediate demand to take it home and wash it.

Peters, however well meaning, did not help in his introduction, immediately announcing to the two players who normally took free-kicks and corners that from then on the new kid would handle all the set pieces. For a shy nineteen-year-old it could all have gone wrong and might have convinced Ferguson that Beckham, who he already regarded as a late developer, might not develop at all.

Something else that might have jarred with the old hands was the build-up from the local media. Before he had played a game, the *Lancashire Evening Post* devoted a full-page feature in its news section to 'the next Bobby Charlton'. Quite who had burdened Beckham with that tag was unclear, but Charlton, as a former Preston manager, had been persuaded to offer a few quotes, telling readers

> he's become a great young player ... with potentially a great future ahead of him. Unfortunately we [United] just haven't got the fixtures and Alex felt he would be better suited to go out and get some competitive edge playing first-team football.

The same paper carried one of the first public indications that Beckham, shy or not, was a media natural. After watching Preston draw 2-2 at Walsall, he struck just the right note: 'I'm here to learn as much as I can. I'm taking nothing for granted. The boss wants me to get as much experience as I can and he's hoping it will harden me up a bit. I know I've got to be worth my place in the side.'

Usefully, there were immediate chances to impress teammates and supporters alike. Joining up on the Monday, he played for the reserves against Mansfield Town two days later and was rewarded with a place on the substitutes' bench for the weekend game at home to Doncaster Rovers. The local paper marked the occasion with an 'exclusive David Beckham poster'.

Preston: Vaughan, Fensome, Kidd, Moyes, Sharp, Cartwright, Davey, Bryson, Lancashire, Conroy, Raynor (Beckham, 46).
Doncaster: Suckling, Kirby, Wilcox, Swailes, Hackett, Harper, Barbin, Schofield, Jones, Norbury, Finlay.
Attendance: 9,624.

The first surprise for Beckham was to look at the Doncaster line-up and discover an old friend. Ryan Kirby was a fellow East Londoner, eight months older, who had played in the Ridgeway Rovers boys team with him, coached by Ryan's father Steve, and then alongside him for Waltham Forest Schools and Essex. Released by Arsenal without making the first team, he moved north and immediately established himself as Rovers' regular right-back.

They would have plenty to talk about after the game, in which the visitors, fifth in the table, led against the run of play with a header by Graeme Jones. Having sat and winced at Fourth Division tackling for 45 minutes, Beckham was brought on for the second half, at which point, according to the *Post,* 'suddenly things started to buzz'.

Within a couple of minutes, Simon Davey, a new signing from Carlisle United, equalised and 9 minutes later the Preston players taken off set-piece duties could hardly complain when Beckham put the ball down for a corner and swung it straight into the net. Doncaster's goalkeeper Perry Suckling told *The Sun* some years later, 'He hit it quite fast and the ball was heading seven or eight yards from my goal so I decided to go for it. But, as I did, the ball whipped in and curled over my head.'

Alas for the excited home supporters, Russell Wilcox headed an equaliser as snow began to fall, leaving Preston 2 points behind the play-off places in ninth place. 'I enjoyed it but it would have been better if we'd won,' Beckham told reporters.

A first win bonus was not long in coming, followed by a second as Preston made the most of a run of home games. Against Fulham, who were one place above them, Beckham scored the decisive third goal in a 3-2 win with the sort of curling free-kick he would make his trademark, and the following Saturday there was jubilation as Lancashire rivals Bury, also chasing promotion, were drubbed 5-0.

A long away trip to Exeter brought another win, in front of barely 2,000 people, and four days later at Lincoln Beckham was credited with his third assist in four games, allowing Ryan Kidd to equalise in a 1-1 draw.

By the end of March, Preston had won three and drawn two of his five games, moving into the top six. Their manager's worst fears were realised, however, when he rang Ferguson to request an extension of the month's loan and was told that Beckham was required back at Old Trafford.

The tribute from Peters amid his personal disappointment was fulsome: 'David has made a significant contribution during his month here. He's fitted in superbly. It's a blow, because he gave us something special. His ability at set pieces is unbelievable – he's possibly the best in the country.'

Preston finished fifth and would have loved to have 'the new Bobby Charlton' for the play-offs. But Bury extracted revenge, beating them over two legs before losing the final, and by then David Beckham was at last a Premiership player.

Manchester United 0 Leeds United 0
Premiership (Old Trafford)
2 April 1995

Brief as it was, the month at Deepdale had exactly the effect United wanted for Beckham: offering regular football of a higher standard, toughening him up in a man's world and reminding him of what a privileged life Manchester United footballers led. He enjoyed it so much that he joined Preston manager Peters in asking Ferguson for an extension, to be turned down for reasons that only became apparent later that week – a Premiership debut and an FA Cup semi-final were beckoning.

At a crucial time of the season, with United falling behind Kenny Dalglish's Blackburn Rovers at the top of the table, the normal occupant of the right-wing berth, Andrei Kanchelskis, had upset Ferguson with his sullen attitude, a transfer request and newspaper criticism of the manager that cost him a week's wages. He then claimed to be injured and so, from playing at Lincoln City on 26 March in front of 5,487 people, David Beckham was suddenly thrust into a first Premiership match at home to the hated Leeds United in front of eight times as many.

It was a crucial game. Blackburn, the previous season's runners-up and a new force with Jack Walker's money, Dalglish's leadership and Alan Shearer's goals, had won the previous day to go 6 points clear. Leeds, although they had not been able to build on their 1992 championship win, were still a top six side and had beaten United at Elland Road in September, despite a penalty from Cantona, who suffered serious abuse. His absence did little to lighten the tension surrounding the return game.

Manchester United: Schmeichel, G Neville, Keane, Pallister, Irwin, Beckham, Ince, McClair, Giggs, Hughes, Cole.
Leeds United: Lukic, Kelly, Wetherall, Pemberton, Dorigo, R Wallace (Worthington, 88), Palmer, McAllister, Couzens, Deane (Whelan, 83), Yeboah.
Attendance: 43,712.

As Beckham admitted later, the game – rather like United's season – was an anticlimax. A hot April afternoon did not help and there was little excitement for the Sky TV audience.

According to *The Guardian's* report, 'Although the 19-year-old Beckham, recalled from Preston, did well on his Premiership debut, he could not be expected to provide the service that Cole has come to expect from Kanchelskis.'

Ferguson claimed, 'I think we should have won, we were very, very unlucky,' and took out some of his frustration on the Russian Football Union, who he criticised for giving Kanchelskis eight painkilling injections earlier in the week so he could play in the Euro 96 qualifier against Scotland.

For Beckham it was an acceptable debut, which left his father even more excited than he was. As his dad recorded later,

> Seeing him make that long walk out of the tunnel and onto the pitch is still one of the proudest moments of my life. In truth the game was a scrappy 0-0 draw but David did pretty well. After the game I saw David and I struggled for words to explain just what I felt about it. I just went up to him, gave him a cuddle and a kiss and said 'Well done, mate. That was brilliant.'

The performance earned him a part in four of the next five games, starting with a lively FA Cup semi-final against Crystal Palace at Villa Park. With Steve Bruce suspended, Roy Keane again played at centre-half for a tie that finished 2-2 after extra-time. Beckham started the game and was replaced later by Nicky Butt.

Tensions, already high because of the Cantona incident three months earlier, were inflamed when it emerged that a Palace supporter had been killed at a Walsall pub before the match. Keane did nothing to calm things down in the replay at the same venue three days later, getting himself sent off for stamping on Gareth Southgate in a 2-0 United victory watched by fewer than 18,000 amid a subdued atmosphere. This time Butt played and Beckham did not get on, but he came on in the subsequent 4-0 win at Leicester, started the goalless draw at home to Chelsea and was used again in a 3-2 win at Coventry.

The dropped points in those Old Trafford games proved costly, even when Ferguson cranked up the psychological pressure on Dalglish and Blackburn, who suddenly faltered. From holding an 8-point lead with six games to play, the upstart Lancastrians won only one match out of four. Going into the final day they led by 2 points, but with an inferior goal difference and so needed to win at Liverpool, where some home supporters were tempted to hope their own side lost, rather than hand United the title. In the event Blackburn were beaten 2-1 by a last-minute goal, but Ferguson's team could not find the winning goal they needed at West Ham, being held 1-1. Rovers were champions by a point.

For the cup final a week later, in which Gary Neville and Butt played the whole game and Scholes came on as a substitute, Beckham would get only a day out at Wembley rather than any active participation. The 1-0 defeat by Everton's self-styled 'Dogs of War', who had finished in the bottom eight of the Premiership, was hugely disappointing for United and confirmed a furious Ferguson in his determination to shake up the squad, which would prove to be highly controversial but very much to the benefit of the Beckham generation.

In a dramatic summer, Cantona, banned until September, had to be persuaded to withdraw a transfer request, Kanchelskis (a week after the season began) and Paul Ince were sold, as per the manager's wishes, and Mark Hughes left, against them. No replacements were signed and a furious Ferguson discovered that the *Manchester Evening News* was running a poll asking whether he should remain manager.

Beckham would presumably have voted in favour, although – still reacting more like a supporter than a new first-team squad member – he admitted to being astonished by the departures:

> There weren't many better players anywhere in Europe; but Mark Hughes, Paul Ince and Andrei Kanchelskis were leaving Old Trafford. I still remember how upset I was when I found out that Mark, in particular, was leaving. I was surprised, too: like most United supporters my first reaction was to wonder what the manager was doing.

Wisely, he did not dare ask, although the reasoning behind releasing Kanchelskis and Ince would have been comfort. As Ferguson put it,

> I was confident that centre midfield would be filled by Nicky Butt and I was reassured by the promise of David Beckham. He was a late developer but was coming into the reckoning and although I wasn't sure whether he would be operating wide on the right or in central midfield, he was certain to be an increasingly important member of the squad. There was also Paul Scholes, who could attack from deep positions.

Neville, every bit the fan like Beckham, admitted to being 'as stunned as any Stretford Ender' on hearing the news of Hughes' departure. But like his friend he immediately recognised how Kanchelskis's' move to Everton had opened up a vacancy on the right wing:

> Becks … had started to come through, stronger and better after a loan spell at Preston, and already plenty of people were taking notice of his technical prowess. He could hit a brilliant pass off any part of his foot – spinning, dipping, a low grass-cutter or whipped into the box. And game after game you've never seen anyone cover so much ground.

Aston Villa 3 Manchester United 1
Premiership (Villa Park)
19 August 1995

It was the game that would become famous for one sound-bite, still being revived every Saturday night almost twenty years later as *Match Of The Day* celebrated its fiftieth birthday in 2014/15. To the delight of Manchester United supporters, it was uttered by an old Liverpool foe, who never lived it down.

Yet when the elegant and eloquent Alan Hansen, analysing Manchester United's defeat by Aston Villa on the opening day of the season, declared 'you can't win anything with kids', there were few people inside or outside football prepared to disagree with him – even Ferguson, who knew full well he would need more of his senior professionals back, whether or not he spent some of the club's money on new ones, as Hansen and many others were urging.

Convinced that he could use the younger generation to cover for Ince, Kanchelskis and even Hughes, the manager had not bargained for injuries and further suspensions before the start of the new season, which meant that as well as that trio he was also missing Steve Bruce, Ryan Giggs and Andy Cole for a tricky first fixture. A few months earlier those six players had all been first-choice starters in the side that was not far away from a second successive Double.

So against a good Villa team under Brian Little, which would finish fourth that season, United fielded both Neville brothers, Butt and Scholes, with Beckham and John O'Kane among the substitutes. Half of the fourteen players involved (only three substitutes were named in those days) were therefore aged twenty-two or under.

Aston Villa: Bosnich, Ehiogu, McGrath, Southgate, Charles, Taylor, Draper, Townsend, Wright, Milosevic (Johnson, 52), Yorke (Scimeca, 88).
Manchester United: Schmeichel, Parker, Pallister (O'Kane, 59), G. Neville, P. Neville (Beckham, 46), Butt, Keane, Sharpe, Irwin, McClair, Scholes.
Attendance: 34,655.

If there was a surprise – and a mistake – other than the number of youngsters included, it was matching Villa's wing-back system, with Phil Neville and Denis Irwin on the flanks in roles they were hardly accustomed to. Ferguson tacitly acknowledged as much at half-time, changing to a more familiar back four by bringing on Beckham for the younger Neville.

By then the damage was done, with Villa, extraordinarily, three goals to the good. Ian Taylor, a popular local lad, arrived from midfield in the 14th minute to prod Gary Charles's ball past Schmeichel. In the 27th minute another midfielder, Mark Draper, finished a lovely five-man move by converting Savo Milosevic's pass and only 10 minutes later Schmeichel brought down the big Yugoslav striker and Dwight Yorke, later to become a United hero, swept in the resulting penalty.

As Colin Malam wrote in the next day's *Sunday Telegraph,*

> At half-time yesterday on a hot summer's afternoon at Villa Park the rest of the season must have stretched ahead of Manchester United like a veritable furnace. Since they were three goals down and totally outplayed, their pre-season strategy of relying more heavily on youth rather than before appeared to be in flames.

Significantly, he added, 'A vastly improved second half performance not only salvaged United's pride but could easily have brought them three or four goals of their own.'

In fact, only one materialised, but it showed the nation what Beckham could do: Taking a pass from Irwin some 25 yards out, he controlled the ball instantly, stepped forward and hit a perfect shot into the top corner of the net for his first League goal. In the context of the game it was too late to matter and only one United player bothered congratulating him, while in the dressing room afterwards Ferguson castigated him for charging all over the place instead of holding his position.

Sitting miserably at home watching *Match of the Day,* Beckham heard Hansen, one season into a twenty-year stint as a BBC pundit, declare when questioned by Des Lynam,

> obviously three players have departed. The trick is always to buy when you're strong. So he [Ferguson] needs to buy players, simple as that. You can't win anything with kids. You look at that line-up today and Aston Villa at quarter past two when they get the team-sheet, it's just gonna give them a lift. And it'll happen every time he plays the kids. He's got to buy players, simple as that. The trick of winning the Championship is having strength in depth. They just haven't got it.

It was the last line, rather than the more famous quote, that proved to be wrong. Ferguson knew perfectly well that an Under-23 team could not win the title back. Stubbornly, however, the only players he brought in during the rest of the season were a seventeen-year-old York City goalkeeper, Nick Culkin (who would play under one minute of League football when coming on as a substitute at Arsenal in injury time four years later), Tony Coton, a more experienced goalkeeper who did not play at all, and William Prunier, a French central defender supposed to be on trial, who was thrust into two Premiership games amid an injury crisis over the new year and consequently qualifies for inclusion in many people's idea of a worst ever United XI.

Ferguson, believing as he did that BBC television's sports department was staffed by Liverpool fans, naturally bridled at Hansen's criticism and the tone of much of the newspaper reporting, which included the *Mail on Sunday*'s assessment:

> Manchester United scrambled for the sanctuary of Old Trafford last night in a state of shock and confusion. Baffled supporters believed they had witnessed the worst possible scenario by the contentious decisions of manager Alex Ferguson to allow popular players to leave the club. But nothing could have prepared them for the embarrassment of witnessing their beloved United being teased and tormented at Villa Park.

Observers prepared to look for positives found some in the second-half performance, as *The Daily Telegraph*, echoing its Sunday sister paper, pointed out: 'United should be commended for raising their pace, most notably through Beckham, whose fast feet and positive approach are a delight to behold.'

A quick run of matches before the first international break of the season proved to be just what was required. As Bruce and Cole returned, with Giggs a regular substitute, United took full advantage to win all three, against West Ham, Wimbledon and away to the champions Blackburn, where Beckham scored the winning goal and took another step into adulthood by daring to shout back at Roy Keane.

Chelsea 1 Manchester United 2
FA Cup Semi-Final (Villa Park)
31 March 1996

If a good run of League results changed the mood after the Aston Villa defeat, there were soon disappointments in two of the three cup competitions. In September, Ferguson misjudged the threat posed by lowly York City for the home leg of a second round League Cup tie, and his weakened team suffered a humiliating 3-0 defeat. A 3-1 victory in the return was therefore insufficient to avoid elimination.

The same month United drew 0-0 in Russia with the little known Rotor Volvograd, but in the second leg not even Peter Schmeichel's headed goal after charging up-field for a corner could prevent a similar fate, this time on away goals after a 2-2 draw.

Beckham played in all four games and a had a run of six successive League matches after the Villa game, dropping down to substitute when Eric Cantona made his long-awaited return after eight months for no less a fixture than Liverpool's visit to Old Trafford. True to form, the Frenchman scored from a penalty to earn a 2-2 draw, celebrating by swinging round one of the stanchions on David James' goal.

United's League form was inconsistent and with Kevin Keegan's Newcastle making the running and no more European involvement, the FA Cup assumed serious significance again. Sunderland, chasing promotion from the First Division, forced a draw at Old Trafford before losing the replay, after which Reading, Manchester City and Southampton were beaten to earn a semi-final against Chelsea, back at Villa Park.

Conscious of not overplaying Beckham, Ferguson had left him out of those last three rounds, but to his delight he was back in for the semi. Growing up fast, David had bought a three-storey townhouse near Ryan Giggs in Worsley, where his parents stayed the night before the game, with Ted, habitually as nervous as his son – if not more so – unable to sleep.

Chelsea: Hitchcock, Duberry, Myers, Lee (Furlong, 87), Clarke (Johnsen, 39), Gullit, Burley, Wise, Phelan (Peacock, 65), Hughes, Spencer.
Manchester United: Schmeichel, P. Neville, May, G. Neville, Sharpe, Beckham, Keane, Butt, Giggs, Cantona, Cole.
Attendance: 38,421.

Chelsea were again in the bottom half of the Premiership table, which did not seem right for a team of such ability. Glenn Hoddle, who had only just stopped playing, was in his final season as their manager before taking charge of England from Terry Venables following Euro 96. Ruud Gullit, who would succeed him at Stamford Bridge, was still in the side and Mark Hughes had everything to prove to his old club. Hughes was one of the nine players from the two teams who had been involved in the FA Cup Final between them two years earlier that United had won 4-0, when he scored one of the goals.

The tone for a thrilling and much closer tie was set early on when Beckham hit the post with a fine effort from a cross by Giggs, but 10 minutes before half-time United found themselves behind. As Peter Fitton of *The Sun* described it, 'For once United's superkids were in a dither as that human battering ram called Sparky (Hughes) rumbled down on top of them. The rampaging Welshman left young Beckham in a heap and went steaming on his way.'

With David left in that rueful heap, possibly feeling he had been fouled, Hughes crossed for Gullit to head in. Up in the main stand Ted Beckham exchanged nervous glances with his neighbour Neville Neville, the oddly named father of the Manchester United brothers, who were both playing in a back line thrown together in the absence of its injured senior members, Steve Bruce and Gary Pallister. Phil was at right-back, Gary in the centre with David May, and Lee Sharpe, normally a winger, was at left-back; the brothers had both been found wanting for the goal.

After Cantona struck a volley against a post, the game turned on two moments just before the hour. In the 55th minute, Beckham set Phil Neville away to cross from the right, the Norwegian defender Erland Johnsen failed to clear, Cantona headed back towards goal and Andy Cole, who had not scored for six games, broke his duck from a foot out.

Only 4 minutes later, Chelsea's Scottish midfielder Craig Burley became the reluctant fall guy, badly under hitting a backpass from just inside his own half. Beckham, onto it immediately, raced away from a struggling Terry Phelan, who had unwisely come back onto the pitch after straining a muscle, and veered slightly further to his right than he intended before cutting the ball back perfectly across the goalkeeper and just inside the far post for his first FA Cup goal.

There was still much excitement to come. With Chelsea throwing on attacking substitutes in Gavin Peacock and Paul Furlong, Schmeichel came out of goal to thwart Gullit, and as the ball fell for John Spencer outside the penalty area, Cantona of all people was brilliantly positioned to head his fierce shot off the line. At the other end, Andy Myers cleared off the line from Cole, before Beckham, from an identical position to his 25-yard goal in the League game at Villa Park, struck a similar shot just too high.

As the scorer of what proved to be the winning goal, he would have his share of the headlines, although it was Cantona that a smiling Ferguson immediately headed for in a rare incursion onto the pitch at the final whistle.

'Glory boy David fires Fergie back to Wembley' read the front of *The Sun*'s football supplement the next day. 'Young David Beckham seized his chance with veteran assurance,' wrote the paper's chief sportswriter John Sadler, while Ferguson told reporters, 'Beckham has been one of our best players today. It's difficult to keep him out of the team. But I still feel he's getting stronger. I think in the next two years he's going to be become a top player. He just has to show patience.'

With Liverpool beating Aston Villa 3-0 in the other semi-final at Old Trafford, the nation had the final it wanted between two of the Premiership's top three teams. Robbie Fowler, that old adversary of Beckham's from way back in Under-16 days (see Chapter 1), was Liverpool's hero with two goals and had just been voted the Professional Footballers' Association Young Player of the Year, ahead of the United contingent. *The Independent* linked the two youngsters in its semi-final coverage, headlining 'Young, gifted and back' as their goals took the respective teams to Wembley.

Football correspondent Glenn Moore wrote from Villa Park 'The feeling that it was to be United's day, which had seemed in doubt when Beckham and Cantona struck a post each in the first period, intensified when Roy Keane escaped being sent off for the second successive semi-final.'

Keane, also dismissed playing for the Republic of Ireland four days earlier, had caught Dennis Wise in the face after the Chelsea captain argued with Beckham, prompting a famous Ferguson line when asked about the incident: 'Dennis Wise could start a row in an empty house.'

The following day's *Sun* featured an interview with several of Beckham's old school friends and his father, who told a story about David, still the star-struck teenager rather than the star, wanting Hristo Stoichkov's autograph when United played Barcelona a year earlier. After the Cup semi-final he reported, 'I didn't say anything and he knew that said everything, because I'm his biggest critic. We're more like mates than father and son.'

According to *The Daily Telegraph*, Ferguson telephoned the family following that article, asking them not to expose David to too much publicity. It was proving increasingly difficult to keep him out of the papers.

Middlesbrough 0 Manchester United 3
Premiership (Riverside Stadium)
5 May 1996

The patience that Ferguson was demanding of Beckham proved unnecessary as United closed in on a third title in the four years of the Premiership. From the Cup semi-final onwards, he would start every game as what was once Newcastle's formidable lead at the top was slowly whittled away.

During a bad run in December, United lost successive games to old rivals Liverpool and Leeds and were 10 points behind Keegan's exciting team ahead of the Christmas meeting between the two at Old Trafford. It was another game in which Bruce and Pallister were both missing and one that United had to win. They did so, 2-0, with goals by Cole and Keane, achieving a victory that Ferguson later pinpointed as the key to regaining their title.

The return at St James' Park in March was hardly less important, but there was a psychological element to it. While Newcastle had just begun dropping points, United were flying after five successive wins, the last of them by 6-0 away to Bolton, with Beckham among the scorers. After an occasional game's rest he was back in the side at Newcastle, where Peter Schmeichel defied all the home team's efforts and Eric Cantona volleyed the only goal to end Newcastle's 100 per cent home record.

Cantona had embarked on a run of scoring in six consecutive games and the gap was down to a single point, although United had played a game more. Newcastle's games in hand kept the chase intriguing, even when they lost four out of six in the spring, culminating in an epic 4-3 defeat at Liverpool. Then United wobbled, losing at Southampton, where Beckham and his teammates were told at half-time to change out of their grey shirts into blue ones; Ferguson said a lack of visibility was contributing to the 3-0 deficit.

The manager indulged in another piece of psychology when he publicly expressed the hope that Leeds, who had pushed his team all the way before Keane's goal beat them at Old Trafford, would fight just as hard in their next game, away to Newcastle. They did so, in again losing 1-0, and the often emotional Keegan lost his cool in a Sky television interview, claiming Ferguson had gone down in his estimation and that he would 'love it, love it!' if Newcastle could snatch the title.

Alas for them, Newcastle's last game in hand was a Thursday night match at Nottingham Forest, where they could only draw 1-1 against a team United had just beaten 5-0 in their final home game, Beckham scoring twice.

Had Newcastle won at the City Ground, the teams would have been level on points going into the final Sunday of the League season. As it was, United knew that with a superior goal difference, a draw away to Middlesbrough would make them champions, whatever Newcastle managed at home to Tottenham.

Middlesbrough: Walsh, Cox, Pearson, Whyte, Branco (Moore, 73), Vickers, Barmby, Pollock (Stamp 57), Juninho, Fjortoft, Mustoe.
Manchester United: Schmeichel, Irwin, May, Pallister, P. Neville, Beckham, Butt, Keane, Giggs, Scholes (Cole, 54), Cantona.
Attendance: 29,922.

Having been involved before in dramatic last-day finishes, and with others to come, Ferguson and United were perfectly happy to settle for coming through one successfully in such straightforward style. Offered the possibility of such an outcome on the night of that opening day embarrassment at Villa Park, they would undoubtedly have chewed off hands to take it.

The greatest danger as their supporters headed to Teesside appeared to be complacency. Middlesbrough, under the former Old Trafford legend Bryan Robson, had won promotion the previous season and been in the Premiership's top six during the autumn, with little Brazilian Juninho pulling most of the strings. Since Christmas, however, they had collapsed, winning only two games out of eighteen. As soon as the maths became apparent after Newcastle's draw in Nottingham, bookmakers made United 10-1 on to become champions.

The best that could be said for Newcastle's prospects was that the pressure weighing them down for the past six months and more had shifted elsewhere, like most of the publicity. The day before the final games, *The Times* had a leading article, no less, about Cantona, 'the one Gallic soul whose British admirers can be counted in their millions'. Already named Footballer of the Year (although the PFA members, voting earlier, went for Newcastle's Les Ferdinand), he would have a quiet game against Middlesbrough, which as it turned out hardly mattered.

The paper's football correspondent Rob Hughes wrote, 'Middlesbrough threatened for only a moment or two ... [and] never looked likely to be only the second team in 22 league and cup games to defeat Ferguson's side.'

Predictably Juninho was the main source of irritation, setting up an early chance for Neil Cox and a later one for Nick Barmby, but the key was David May becoming the unlikely first goalscorer. After 13 minutes, Giggs sent over a corner and the centre-half, playing instead of Bruce, headed his first goal for a year.

Another Giggs corner brought a second goal in the 53rd minute, Cole cleverly hooking the ball over his shoulder with his first touch after coming on to replace Scholes.

With Middlesbrough now needing three goals, Newcastle struggling against Tottenham and – even better – Manchester City about to suffer relegation, United's following of 2,300 fans were in full voice.

The icing on their cake, ensuring where all the headlines went, was a run starting 35 yards out by Giggs, who left defenders trailing and swerved a shot with the outside of his foot past the former United goalkeeper Gary Walsh.

Cantona, *The Times* said prophetically, was 'no doubt conserving something for the FA Cup final next Saturday'. The paper's front page included the headline 'Manchester divided by football joy and grief', a reference to City's demotion to the First Division after a 2-2 draw with Liverpool.

Beckham had his first championship medal, having scored eight times and played in thirty-three of the thirty-eight League games. He had built himself up physically with a lot of weight training, having been outmuscled in a number of early games against people like West Ham's Julian Dicks and Forest's Stuart Pearce, and with the responsibility of his own home and car was maturing off the field too.

Having so many survivors around from the youth team of three and four years earlier obviously helped, and their statistics that season were impressive too: Gary Neville and Nicky Butt had more than thirty League games each, Scholes twenty-six (ten goals) and Phil Neville twenty-four. All of which was not a bad riposte to Alan Hansen.

Now for the FA Cup. What a jubilant Beckham did not know amid the Sunday night championship celebrations was that Ferguson would be contemplating whether to leave him out of the final.

Liverpool 0 Manchester United 1
FA Cup Final (Wembley)
11 May 1996

Looking up at his parents in the stand at Villa Park after the semi-final, David Beckham had tears in his eyes. They might have come back if he knew about the discussion Alex Ferguson was having with United's coaches and senior players two days before the final against Liverpool.

As well as drawing at Old Trafford on the occasion of Cantona's comeback, Roy Evans' team had beaten United 2-0 at Anfield and Ferguson revealed later, 'I was slightly worried by their system of playing three centre-backs, with wing-backs pushing forward and Stan Collymore floating from up front to deeper positions and Steve McManaman releasing himself from midfield.'

Ferguson contemplated matching up by also using wing-backs, which as on the opening day of the season could well have meant Beckham dropping out. He involved Schmeichel, the back four, Cantona and Keane in the discussion and found them unhappy with the idea. Cantona suggested using Keane as a shield in front of the back four, which the manager happily accepted.

His selection dilemma was then limited to which of the Nevilles should play at full-back – Phil won – whether to recall his captain Steve Bruce or leave David May in, and whether Cole or Scholes should start as the main striker. The goals that May and Cole had scored at Middlesbrough did them no harm and they were both given the nod, which meant Cantona would be captain.

Liverpool had boldly named their team the day before the game, with Phil Babb, the young Irish international, joining Mark Wright and John Scales as central defenders, while Jamie Redknapp was preferred in midfield to Michael Thomas.

Liverpool: James, Wright, Scales, Babb, McAteer, Redknapp, Barnes, Jones, (Thomas, 86), McManaman, Collymore (Rush, 74), Fowler.
Manchester United: Schmeichel, Irwin, May, Pallister, P. Neville, Beckham (G. Neville, 90), Keane, Butt, Giggs, Cantona, Cole (Scholes, 64).
Attendance: 79,007.

Wembley had been a special place for Beckham ever since his first visit, for a schoolboy international at the age of seven. The reason for his tears of happiness after the semi-final was a realisation that he would be playing there in the Cup Final for Manchester United.

He had been present, aged fifteen, when United drew an epic final 3-3 with Crystal Palace in 1990 and had shared the joy of the 1994 victory over Chelsea and the pain of an unexpected 1-0 defeat by Everton in the 1995 final. Now here they were for the third successive year.

Ted Beckham was so excited by the prospect that he insisted on taking Sandra all the way from London to Manchester the day before, so they could stay at David's house then join the other players' families in returning on a special train before checking in at the Royal Lancaster Hotel near the Football Association headquarters.

The familiar feelings of pride as his son passed each of these new milestones welled up again: 'My mind drifted back to those days back at Ridgeway Rovers, all the long hours we'd spent together on cold winter evenings practising and practising, and I felt so proud of what he'd achieved.'

Even this proudest of fathers, who would be as thrilled as anyone by the eventual result, had to admit it was not much of a game. The heat, tension and a slow pitch might all have been contributory factors and for many neutrals the day is still remembered, if at all, for Liverpool's cringeworthy white suits.

Cantona's admirers also have happy memories of the match, and so do the Beckhams – for David's part in the Frenchman's match-winning goal just as extra-time appeared to be looming. Again, however, his participation was under threat as he lined up a corner in the 86th minute.

Although the manager has subsequently described Beckham as 'probably the best striker of a dead ball I have ever come across,' he had been unimpressed that day by David's set-pieces and told his assistant Brian Kidd that if this next corner landed harmlessly in the arms of Liverpool's goalkeeper David James, Beckham would be substituted.

It almost did, but swung just far enough away towards the penalty spot and James, coming to claim it under pressure from May, could only punch as far as the lurking Cantona, who volleyed it back past him for the only goal.

Beckham was almost immediately taken off anyway, for an extra defender, but hardly minded as it was his great friend Gary Neville. As Cantona lifted the Cup, completing his redemption sixteen months after Selhurst Park, Beckham turned to Neville and said 'can you believe this is happening to us?'

All he remembers of the aftermath in the dressing room is 'screaming, singing and laughing' as United celebrated becoming the first club ever to win a second League and Cup Double, which they had done in the space of three years.

So for the second Monday running, the big picture for the newspapers was Cantona holding up a trophy and this time he was the story. *The Times* said,

> The transformation of Eric Cantona from social outcast to a man able to turn the other cheek while being spat upon on the steps to the Royal Box at Wembley appears so complete one wonders whether some kind of mind altering therapy has been at work.

Under the headline 'Moment of genius decides moribund final', the match was described elsewhere in the paper as one of 'turgid incompetence'. The goal 'provided you stayed awake for the moment ... was exceptional indeed'.

Roy Evans admitted Liverpool had arrived on back of 'a couple of indifferent performances' and said his young players needed 'a more professional attitude'. He may well have had United's kids in mind.

Whatever Ferguson thought about his corner-kicks, Beckham had reason to feel satisfied with his own performance, which included bringing a fine save from James early on and setting Cantona up to force another in the second half.

Brian Clough, retired from management but contributing a ghosted column for the *News of the World*, rated the match 'a dreadful bore' but added, 'young David Beckham was lively and direct', and in the same paper, Arsenal's Ian Wright added of him, 'A real quality prospect, he won key tackles and showed he has a great attitude on the big occasion.'

The big occasions, however, were only just beginning.

12

Wimbledon 0 Manchester United 3
Premiership (Selhurst Park)
17 August 1996

A little surprisingly for such a football fanatic and patriot, David Beckham took little notice of Euro 96 – the tournament when football was supposed to be coming home, but which ended with German fans and players singing the number one hit written in the hope of becoming England's victory anthem. On holiday in Sardinia, reflecting that 'we really had achieved something [and] Gary, Phil, Nicky, Scholesy and myself all had the first medals of a professional career to prove it', he swam and sunbathed rather than watching television, before being thrown back into pre-season training at United.

Steve Bruce, no doubt disappointed at missing out on the climax to the season, had reluctantly been allowed to leave for Birmingham City on a free transfer and replaced by Norwegian Ronny Johnsen, one of a crop of foreign players arriving; others included Karel Poborsky, a star of Euro 96's surprise finalists, the Czech Republic, Jordi Cruyff, the son of Johan, and a little Norwegian striker called Ole Gunnar Solskjaer.

As had happened two years earlier, the FA decided that United should contest the Charity Shield match against the League runners-up, and Ferguson's team duly beat Newcastle 4-0, Beckham joining Roy Keane in scoring in the last 5 minutes. It was an encouraging warm up a week before a match and a goal that, without exaggeration, would change his life.

Many teams would have regarded an away game against Wimbledon as a daunting first League fixture. Under Joe Kinnear the Londoners were no mugs, neither the Crazy Gang nor the long-ball merchants of old; by the start of December that season they would stand second in the Premiership, eventually finishing eighth after beating Arsenal, Chelsea and Liverpool.

Selhurst Park, where they had moved five years earlier, was admittedly a less intimidating arena than cramped and rudimentary Plough Lane, which they had left to share with Crystal Palace. Wimbledon attracted perhaps 10,000 of their own supporters, which left room for some 15,000 or more when United and the big London clubs visited. Sure enough there was a crowd of over 25,000 on a sunny day to welcome in the new season.

Wimbledon: Sullivan, Cunningham, Perry, McAllister, Thatcher (Ardley, 77), Earle, Jones, Leonhardsen, Holdsworth (Ekoku, 77), Gayle (Harford, 83), Clarke.
Manchester United: Schmeichel, Irwin, May, Pallister, P. Neville, Beckham, Keane, Butt (Johnsen, 39), Cruyff, Scholes, Cantona (McClair, 75).
Attendance: 25,786.

It was a day for short sleeves and many United fans were delighted to be wearing T-shirts bearing the legend 'you can't win anything with kids'. The Double winners, metaphorically rolling up their sleeves, were dominant from the start and went ahead in the 27th minute when Beckham began a move carried on by Keane and touched square by Butt for Cantona to score from 15 yards.

United made light of losing Nicky Butt with concussion shortly before the interval and were coasting by the time Denis Irwin scored a rare goal in the 58th minute after a one-two with Keane, who then hit both the bar and post.

With Andy Cole and Ryan Giggs both unavailable, Jordi Cruyff had been given a debut and it was his attempt to chip Wimbledon goalkeeper Neil Sullivan that planted a seed in the mind of Beckham. When Brian McClair passed to him a few minutes later, he decided to emulate the Dutchman, albeit from some 55 yards out, striking the ball up and away with the precision of a leading golfer using a seven iron, as Sullivan suddenly retreated in panic. Patrick Collins wrote in the next morning's *Mail on Sunday*,

> There was a moment of silence when the ball dipped beneath the bar, with 25,000 people catching their breath and blinking their disbelief.
>
> Then David Beckham punched the air and performed a little jig of joy. And a glorious bedlam ensued.
>
> It was a marvellous celebration of a memorable goal. The wit which inspired Beckham to such audacity will surely render him one of the original talents of English football, yet it took something momentous to secure the spotlight on a day when Roy Keane was at his most formidable.

In *The Sunday Telegraph* Clive White wrote, 'The 26,000 crowd stood as one to applaud United's 300th goal in the Premiership, which for sheer audacity will take some beating in the months ahead.'

Ferguson did not think that would happen, suggesting 'we've seen the goal of the season already'. Had the ball not dropped into the net, his mood would have been rather different, for those in United's dug-out at the time reported him saying of a previous attempt, 'if he tries that again, he's off'. Later, telling the story against himself, Ferguson said, 'At the time, David was getting carried away a bit and you are always trying to keep his feet on the ground. When the goal goes in, Kiddo turns to me and says, "We'll have to take him off!"'

Thrilled above all by having Cantona tell him 'what a goal', Beckham did not mind Ferguson ordering him not to talk to *Match of the Day* or anyone else after the game. What not even the all-powerful manager could prevent, however, was the upshot of it all.

As Gary Neville has said, 'It did catapult him onto a different level. I think it went a little bit mad.' For Beckham, looking back seven years later, 'That moment was the start of it all: the attention, the press coverage, the fame, that whole side of what's happened to me since.'

The madness had truly begun and John Motson anticipated the next step in his BBC commentary of the sublime moment: 'That is absolutely phenomenal. David Beckham, surely an England player of the future ...'

13

Moldova 0 England 3
World Cup Qualifying (Chisinau)
1 September 1996

David Beckham was sitting on the sofa at his parents' modest house in Chingford when he learnt via Teletext that he was in the full England squad for the first time. He immediately jumped off it in excitement before telephoning the news to his dad, who was working that day as a gas fitter at a hotel in London.

Although Gary Neville was already an international and brother Phil had one cap, Manchester United's Double winners were otherwise unrepresented in England's squad at Euro 96. Beckham was at least on the FA's radar, having played four times for the Under-18s in the 1992–93 season, and nine times later at Under-21 level, but that limited number of caps (James Milner, for instance, played forty-six times for the Under-21s) confirms Ferguson's view of him as a late developer.

As a schoolboy he had never progressed beyond county level, and the coaches at the FA National School at Lilleshall were among those who felt he was too small (which did not stop them taking Michael Owen a few years later).

Fortunately, Glenn Hoddle was an admirer. He had become England's youngest ever manager, at thirty-eight, after the FA foolishly let Terry Venables slip through their fingers, and had watched three of Beckham's Under-21 games at the 1996 Toulon tournament as well as taking note – how could he not? – of his early season performances at Wembley and Selhurst.

'Beckham is a player who sees the furthest pass first,' Hoddle said of someone who was very much a kindred spirit, adding,

> There are enough around in football who see no further than the nearest ball. If you see the furthest, most penetrative one first, then your options are so much more creative. Beckham has got that ability. He selects his passes in a mature way, way beyond his years. And he has also got an eye for goal, which is a bonus.

So Hoddle named him in the squad to play away to Moldova, as well as club mate Gary Pallister and Everton's Andy Hinchcliffe, although the bigger story for the news media was the recall of Southampton's maverick Matt Le Tissier, who Venables claimed could not be fitted into his system.

Alex Ferguson offered Beckham congratulations while privately wondering whether it was all happening too soon. Protective as ever, just as he had been after the Wimbledon goal, he wanted his player kept away from the media, but the FA put him up for a news conference and in the words of the late Brian Woolnough, football writer at the time for *The Sun* 'he made all the right noises and said all the right things'.

As Woolnough and others pointed out, Beckham was twenty-one – an age at which equally talented players in other countries would already have had a hat-stand full of caps. Taking another step up the ladder, he overcame initial nerves, trained brilliantly and was rewarded with a place in the starting XI as a central midfielder, with Gary Neville a comforting presence as wing-back on his right.

Moldova: Romanenco, Secu, Nani, Testimitanu, Gaidamasciuc, Belous (Siscin, 58), Epureanu, Curtianu, Clescenco, Miterev (Rebeja, 61), Popovici.
England: Seaman, Pallister, Southgate, Pearce, G. Neville, Beckham, Ince, Gascoigne (Batty, 81), Hinchcliffe, Shearer, Barmby (Le Tissier, 81).
Attendance: 15,000.

Moldova were something of an unknown quantity, who would eventually finish bottom of the group, but with Italy and Poland in the same section and only one team earning automatic qualification for the finals in France, it was the sort of game that England needed to win.

They duly did so without any great alarms. In *The Guardian* match report, headlined 'England roll over Moldova', David Lacey wrote,

At least England are on their way. Glenn Hoddle's term of office might have begun a trifle nervously in the Republican Stadium here yesterday evening as his team worked out the new coach's plan of action, but England's scoring habits of Euro 96 did not desert them.

Moldova, clever going forward but defensively naive, were beaten comfortably enough as England stole a march on their World Cup rivals. Two quick goals in the first half, from Nick Barmby and Paul Gascoigne, gave England an unshakeable grip and a third just past the hour from Alan Shearer, the nation's 100th captain, confirmed their mounting superiority.

Of Beckham, Lacey added 'the youngster looked worth another outing', which suggested nobody was necessarily expecting another 114 of them in an England shirt.

Hoddle had stuck with the 3-5-2 formation employed by Venables, although the one adjustment was that he used defenders like Neville and Hinchcliffe in the wing-back positions, where Venables had preferred wingers in Steve McManaman and Darren Anderton.

Early on, the new defensive trio of Pallister, Gareth Southgate and Stuart Pearce were slow to familiarise themselves with each other and Moldova had chances, but Niterev and Popovici wasted them. Testimitanu on the left, where it was more Neville's job than Beckham's to control him, also looked a threat, but as so often the first goal proved important.

In the 24th minute, newcomers Beckham and Hinchcliffe twice switched the play, and Neville, always a willing attacker, crossed for Barmby to score.

A couple of minutes later, Paul Ince, who might have been penalised for a high foot, got away with it and Paul Gascoigne headed in off the bar. Now it was England who were wasting chances, until just after the hour, when Southgate and Neville created an opportunity and Shearer lunged in to score. Towards the end Pearce conceded a penalty for handball, but Testimitanu's shot hit the angle of bar and post.

The verdict of most observers echoed that in *The Guardian* of a job well done without causing any great excitement. Gascoigne was regarded as not fit and off the pace, which would become a theme of the campaign, but in *The Sun,* Martin Samuel wrote of the two debutants, 'Beckham and Andy Hinchcliffe ... played their part in a win which impressed in its efficiency while hardly sending shock waves through the continent.'

Beckham received a mark of 8/10, and the comment 'Took responsibility, looked mature and gave us some lovely 40-yard passes. He is here to stay.'

Hoddle said,

> I thought David did well after the opening ten minutes. He reacted maturely and he is one for the future. I would have liked more composure on the ball and we should have scored more goals. England are not anywhere near playing the way I want to.

The verdict of the man himself was a feeling of belonging straightaway. He would stay in the team as well as the squad for the rest of the qualifying campaign, starting with a Wembley debut for his country in the next game, at home to Poland.

There was another nervous start there, when the visitors revived memories of their famous World Cup performance in denying Sir Alf Ramsey's England in 1973 by taking the lead. Southgate looked especially uncomfortable as the sweeper, but Alan Shearer scored twice as Hoddle's team joined Italy with maximum points from the first two games.

Next up were Georgia, and a defining fixture that Beckham would always remember for reasons that had nothing to do with football.

14

Georgia 0 England 2
World Cup Qualifying (Tbilisi)
9 November 1996

As a young teenager, David Beckham would be practising free-kicks in the park while his friends were off chasing girls. By the time he became a professional with Manchester United, he was able to manage both, in a typically disciplined sort of way.

There was Julie (who later married Phil Neville), and Helen, a pretty Merseysider who was his girlfriend at the time of the 1996 FA Cup Final win over Liverpool and joined his family on the official trip and at the after-match party. Then, six months later, he switched on the television in a hotel in Tbilisi and his life changed forever.

Bored in between training sessions ahead of England's third World Cup qualifying match, Beckham and his regular roommate Gary Neville sought distraction with the TV, where they found the Spice Girls dancing in the desert to their second hit 'Say You'll Be There', with Victoria Adams, aka 'Posh Spice', looking particularly fetching in her unusual desert wear – a black catsuit.

The girls were hardly unknown after seven weeks on top of the charts and David had long ago decided which was his favourite – the one journalistic doyen Brian Glanville has always called 'relatively posh'. Now Beckham told a mildly amused Neville that he just had to meet her. But first, there was a World Cup match to get out of the way.

Georgia: Zoidze, Lobjanidze, Tskhadze, Shelia, Gogichaishvili (Gudushauri, 60), Nemsadze, Kinkladze, Jamarauli, Kobiashvili, Ketsbaia, Aveladze, (Gogrichiani, 52).
England: Seaman, Campbell, Southgate, Adams, Beckham, Ince, Gascoigne, Batty, Hinchcliffe, Ferdinand (Wright, 81), Sheringham.
Attendance: 48,000.

Build-up to the game had been dominated by whether Paul Gascoigne, now at Rangers, would play. A hero at Euro 96 and married soon afterwards, he was having drinking problems and was receiving help from England teammate Tony Adams, who had himself startled the new Arsenal manager Arsene Wenger by admitting to being an alcoholic, and was in daily contact with counsellors.

Glenn Hoddle decided to pick both and neither let him down in a solid England performance. Georgia, entering the World Cup for the first time, had lost their opening group game only 1-0 away to Italy and had talented players in Temur Ketsbaia, who would later join Newcastle, and Manchester City's Georgi Kinkladze, but by the closing minutes their supporters were throwing empty cans and bottles towards the pitch.

Earlier the crowd of almost 50,000 had been more supportive as Tbilisi native Kinkladze did his tricks, but Hoddle, who had warned his midfield players Ince and David Batty not to dive in on him, was gratified by an England goal after only 15 minutes.

Gascoigne volleyed a perfect pass for Les Ferdinand, replacing the injured Alan Shearer, to find Teddy Sheringham, who ran on to score off the foot of a defender. In the 38th minute the same trio combined again for a second goal, Gascoigne and Sheringham sweeping the ball upfield and Ferdinand running on to score.

The *Observer* headline the next day was 'Batty the minder plays a blinder'. The following day's *Daily Mail* gave the Newcastle midfielder an extravagant   10/10 while Beckham, coming close to a first international goal with one 30-yard drive, received a mark of seven and the comment 'Spoiled another progressive performance with a booking. Grows into international football with each game.'

With Batty's inclusion among the central trio alongside Ince and Gascoigne, Beckham's role had changed to becoming one of the wing-backs. It suited his capacity at the time for hard work; shuffling up and back worked well enough and England had 9 points from three games. A satisfied Hoddle said,

> We've now got a psychological advantage when we play Italy in February. I can have a good Christmas now. It was a good all-round display with some fine individual performances. We gave the Georgians a lot of respect. It's not an easy place to come and win but we probably deserved it. Georgi Kinkladze is a superb footballer, but we stopped him playing today. We got the early goal and that gave us a good lift and confidence.

That 'psychological advantage' was lost, however, when Italy, with 6 points from two games, came to Wembley in February and inflicted England's first ever World Cup defeat at the national stadium thanks to a goal by Gianfranco Zola. For various reasons the side showed seven changes from Tbilisi. Beckham was one of the four who kept his place, his best effort on the night being a free-kick well saved by goalkeeper Angelo Peruzzi.

Although some of the changes, like having Ian Walker in goal, were enforced, others were not and Hoddle was widely criticised in, for instance, *The Independent*:

> Perhaps Glenn Hoddle should have given up gambling for Lent. Not on the horses, on the footballers. Last night he risked England's World Cup hopes on the sloping shoulders of Matt Le Tissier. The gamble failed. Hoddle's faith, in this case, was misplaced. Le Tissier had chances but missed them. Alongside, Alan Shearer had barely a sniff at goal and Steve McManaman was shepherded into blind alleys. In defence, the other gamble

– of entrusting the sweeper's role to Sol Campbell – was also exposed. After 19 minutes, Gianfranco Zola broke free of Campbell and Stuart Pearce and, almost inevitably, scored.

Later that month Beckham would have a happier trip to London, scoring in a 1-1 draw at Chelsea to keep United on top of the Premiership and being introduced after the game to the woman he was desperate to meet.

No great fan of either football or those who played it, ('an immoral bunch') Victoria Adams had missed Beckham's spectacular volleyed goal by not wearing her contact lenses. She did, however, recognise him when the Spice Girls manager Simon Fuller performed the introductions, having apparently told her 'I see you with someone famous. What you need is a footballer.'

At a home game against Sheffield Wednesday the following month she was present again with Melanie C and agreed to give David her phone number, which led to a first date, ending up in a Chingford Chinese restaurant not wanting to eat and then getting Mel C out of bed for somewhere to go.

It was an inauspicious start to the relationship, which they could hardly expect to keep quiet for long. If Victoria, at that stage, was the more famous worldwide, David was catching up as United homed in another Premiership title and progressed to within sight of the trophy that they had not won for almost thirty years and now craved above all others – the Champions League.

15

Manchester United 0 Borussia Dortmund 1
(Aggregate 0-2)
Champions League Semi-Final Second Leg
(Old Trafford)
23 April 1997

The European Cup, expanded and rebranded in the early nineties as the Champions League, was dear to Manchester United's heart from its earliest days. It was in that competition that the team devastated by the Munich air disaster of 1958 played their last game, away to Red Star Belgrade, which made the 1968 triumph at Wembley against Benfica all the more emotional, and not just for survivors like Matt Busby and Bobby Charlton.

Alex Ferguson had achieved spectacular European success with Aberdeen by winning the Cup-Winners' Cup and repeated it with United in 1991 (beating Real Madrid and Barcelona in the respective finals), but since then five successive seasons of European football had brought only frustration: elimination in the first round twice, the second round twice and the group stage of the 1994–95 Champions League, when David Beckham made his debut in the competition against Galatasaray.

From the life-changing summer of 1996, however, his experience of continental travel, matches and opponents was suddenly broadened as climbing aboard an aeroplane wearing a United or England blazer became a regular occurrence. On either side of the internationals in Moldova and Georgia came Champions League trips to play Juventus in Turin, Istanbul's Fenerbahce and Rapid Vienna.

Results, both away and at home, were highly unpredictable. At the end of the group stage, in which Beckham played every game, scoring two goals, United's proud unbeaten home record in almost sixty European matches played over forty years had been shattered by both Fenerbahce and Juventus, but by winning in Istanbul and doing the double over Rapid, Ferguson's charges scraped through the section in second place behind the Italians.

Porto, the quarter-final opponents, had an impressive reputation but were demolished 4-0 at Old Trafford, and a goalless draw in the return game meant United were in the last four and fancying their chances against Borussia Dortmund. A 1-0 away defeat in the atmospheric Westfalenstadion was a setback, if hardly a fatal one.

Manchester United: Schmeichel, G. Neville, May (Scholes, 87), Pallister, P. Neville
Beckham, Johnsen, Butt, Cantona, Cole, Solskjaer (Giggs, 57).
Borussia Dortmund: Klos, Kohler, Feiersinger, Kree, Heinrich, Reuter (Tretschok, 24),
Ricken (Zorc, 61), Moller, Lambert, Riedle (Herrlich, 73), Chapuisat.
Attendance: 53,606.

Dortmund, missing five internationals for the second leg, still had a useful looking side
that included Andy Moller, Karl-Heinz Riedle and the future manager of Norwich City
and Aston Villa, Paul Lambert. United had Peter Schmeichel back in goal after missing
the first game, but were without Roy Keane due to suspension.

Failure to score an away goal meant, as ever, that it was important not to concede the
first goal at home, but that was what happened in only the 8th minute. Gary Pallister's
ineffective clearance was picked up by Moller and Schmeichel was beaten when Lars
Ricken's shot took a deflection off Gary Neville.

United poured forward for the rest of the night, as they had to, but chances were
frittered away and as is often the case luck seemed to have gone missing. From a Beckham
free-kick, Ole Gunnar Solskjaer touched the ball in but the Swiss referee ruled that David
May had committed a foul. Late on Andy Cole had the ball in the net, but this time
substitute Giggs was penalised. May headed too high and Cantona delayed too long,
allowing Jurgen Kohler, who was excellent throughout, to rob him.

Cantona 'had a terrible match', according to *The Independent,* which headlined
'United stricken by Ricken' and reported,

> Despite an honourable campaign their cup campaign is over. The goal they conceded
> to Borussia Dortmund in Germany – and the ones they failed to score – put them at a
> disadvantage even before kick-off last night. Seven minutes after, it was trebled when
> Lars Ricken capitalised on defensive sloppiness to put the German champions 2-0 up on
> aggregate. It left United needing to score three times while not conceding once. It was
> too much to ask even though they created enough chances to score twice as many.

Ferguson said,

> I didn't see anything they were better at then us. I don't think losing a goal was such
> a blow because we kept creating chances but it gave Dortmund the comfort to keep
> sticking their heads in and defend with a bit of resolution. I'm not afraid of next season.
> I think we can go one step better. I think it goes without saying that Europe is our aim.

Beckham felt his team had been 'mugged twice', but admitted his direct opponent Jorg
Heinrich was as difficult as anyone he had played against. Improved campaign or not,
the fact was that United had lost twice each to the finalists, Dortmund later taking
advantage of playing in their own country by beating Juventus 3-1 in Munich.

The experience made Beckham and his teammates all the more determined to find some real success in Europe. In the meantime his consolation came in the shape of excellent personal form for club and country, and another Premiership title. It had been a strange League season, during which United briefly seemed to have lost their way when suffering embarrassing defeats by 5-0 at Newcastle and 6-3 at Southampton in the same October week, then losing the next game at home to Chelsea.

The title was confirmed the day after they recovered from 3-1 down to draw with lowly Middlesbrough, and with two games still to play, Beckham broke a drinking curfew for what he claimed was the only time, joining the celebrations at Ben Thornley's house and then enjoying a night on the town.

Thornley and Chris Casper of the Boys of '92 had been particularly unlucky with injuries, playing only two first-team games each, while Beckham appeared more often than any of his contemporaries, even Giggs. He had played in thirty-six League games, missing only two and scoring eight goals, while adding four goals in other competitions to reach double figures, and his burgeoning reputation was reflected in the Professional Footballers' Association award as Young Player of the Year.

Champions League disappointment apart, he felt 'things couldn't have gone much better' for him. Furthermore, despite an initially frosty reception from Victoria's parents ('you're the footballer then are you?' and 'what team do you play for?'), he had decided he was in love. A World Cup was twelve months away – if England could qualify.

16

Italy 0 England 0
World Cup Qualifying Group (Rome)
11 October 1997

The 1997–98 season had an uncomfortable start for Beckham and from Manchester United's perspective did not improve. Despite signing Teddy Sheringham, a fellow Londoner brought up barely a mile away from him, they would eventually end up without a trophy, finishing 1 point behind Double winners Arsenal after leading them at the halfway mark by 13 points; messing up a Champions League quarter-final against Monaco on away goals, and going out of the two domestic cups to opposition as modest as Ipswich Town and Barnsley.

Already shocked by Eric Cantona's dramatic retirement (despite inheriting the Frenchman's coveted number seven shirt against Alex Ferguson's wishes), Beckham found he was only a substitute for the August Charity Shield encounter with Chelsea and the first two League games. It was the first strong hint that Ferguson did not approve of his liaison with Victoria and all the additional publicity it was attracting, with photographers now regularly camped outside his house in Worsley.

Only after coming on for Paul Scholes to score the winning goal at home to Southampton, did he finally win his place back, just in time to make sure he was ready for the crucial international season.

After losing to Italy at Wembley in February, England had beaten Georgia 2-0 then won an important game in Poland, where Italy only drew, by the same score. Alan Shearer and Sheringham, inevitably dubbed the SAS, got the goals on both occasions. In September they romped to a 4-0 home win over Moldova, with Beckham crossing for Scholes to score the opening goal with a brave diving header. He was now so important to England that in the 69th minute Glenn Hoddle substituted him, so as not to risk a booking that would rule him out of the decisive game in Rome.

That assignment suddenly took on a less daunting complexion when Italy again dropped points, drawing 0-0 in Georgia, so that a draw in the final match would be sufficient for England, leaving the Italians in a play-off.

Hoddle detected another of his psychological advantages:

Psychologically there is an edge that has swung around to us now. We don't need to get there to win any more. I've always thought we could go there and win, but it takes the edge away because a draw will do us in the end. The pressure is just a little bit more on them now than on us. The Georgia result was a nice surprise. I didn't expect it. I thought Italy would go there and win. All in all it shows what a good result ours was when we went out there and won 2-0.

England had lost Shearer and Les Ferdinand to injuries, and despite telling his players the team four days beforehand and hoping they would for once keep it quiet, Hoddle played games with the media representatives of both countries. To confuse the Italians, he pulled Beckham out of one training session 10 minutes early, sending him to the dressing room with the doctor, and also asked English sports editors to print one or two either/ors in their predicted teams.

Italy: Peruzzi, Nesta, Costacurta, Cannavaro, Maldini (Benarrivo, 31), Di Livio, Albertini, D Baggio, Zola (Del Piero, 63), Vieri, Inzaghi (Chiesa, 46).
England: Seaman, Campbell, Southgate, Adams, Beckham, Batty, Ince, Gascoigne (Butt, 87), Le Saux, Sheringham, Wright.
Attendance: 81,200.

Even when they received the Italian line-up, with two strikers and Zola as well England were not certain how the home team would play, imagining that the little Chelsea man, reigning Footballer of the Year, would operate just behind Christian Vieri and Filippo Inzaghi. In fact, to their delight, he stationed himself on the left and had a quiet game.

Gascoigne, back at his old Lazio stomping ground, seemed to have his demons under control and was outstanding; he controlled the game from the centre while Ince and Batty protected him, and Beckham and Le Saux worked the flanks.

Beckham was involved in England's two best chances of an encouraging first half. He produced a characteristic diagonal cross to Sheringham, from where the ball was knocked down for Ince – who would later need stitches in his head and play on with a bloodied bandage – to force Peruzzi into a good save. Then he played a one-two with Sheringham and held his head after shooting just over the bar. 'Absolutely top-class football,' co-commentator Andy Gray told the Sky Sports audience.

Much of it was, and with the thousands of England supporters making themselves heard, Italy did not threaten for an hour until Seaman had to save from Enrico Chiesa, who had replaced Inzaghi at the interval. The Dutch referee Mario van der Ende was also doing as well as England could have hoped amid the febrile atmosphere, booking Alessandro del Piero for a dive in the penalty area and then sending off Angelo di Livio for a second serious foul.

In the final minute Ian Wright latched onto a defensive mistake and could have sealed the Italians' fate, but after going round Peruzzi he could only hit the post from a tight angle. Immediately the home side broke for a last time and Vieri should have headed in the cross but put it wide.

'I'd have shot myself if Vieri had scored,' an emotional Wright told reporters. Hoddle said, at what he later described as 'the most enjoyable press conference of my England reign',

> We deserved it. We passed the ball well. It's great for the nation. It's eight years since we qualified and now the hard work starts. I thought we were the best team. We passed the ball well and kept our heads. The whole back five, I can't say anyone was under eight out of ten for effort and the way we played.

The press were in full agreement, praising England's combination of skilful control and dogged determination. Emotions were running high everywhere. Beckham, an England player for barely a year and 'proud to be part of it all', was heading to the World Cup finals and all the dramas that would involve. It seemed inconceivable that Gascoigne, given his performance that night, would not be.

The other thing nobody realised at the time was what Hoddle was going through. Only he knew, as the squad landed at Luton Airport at half past four in the morning, that he was returning home to tell his wife and three children that he was leaving them.

17

Colombia 0 England 2
World Cup Group G (Lens)
26 June 1998

Glenn Hoddle had been a boyhood hero of Beckham's, but by the end of the 1998 World Cup in France his father Ted has said, 'the respect he had for Glenn all but died'.

Hoddle, it is now accepted, came to the hugely demanding job of England manager too early. At thirty-eight, he remains by far the youngest man to take it; only a year before his appointment, confirmed in May 1996, he was still appearing in the Premiership as player-manager of Chelsea. Players who had worked with the amiable Terry Venables found the new regime far less relaxed. 'A big change for us to handle,' David Seaman called it, as extra rules and regulations were introduced. Another player complained that 'training is so bloody serious'.

Given his debut by a man who meant so much to him, Beckham originally had no such concerns, recalling a year later how when he first linked up with England, feeling very nervous, Hoddle took him aside for a chat, which 'meant a lot'.

A first sign of what would prove to be lingering tension with the manager, however, occurred at the end of the 1996–97 season during *Le Tournoi* in France, a useful four-team competition with strong opposition played at World Cup venues. An unnecessary yellow card for retaliation against France meant Beckham had been booked in successive matches and missed out on playing in the last game against Brazil. It brought the first of several lectures, public and private, from Hoddle, who said he had to learn not to react to opponents, referees or hostile crowds.

There was never any doubt that he would be in the squad for France, which in late May had to be cut from twenty-eight to twenty-two at England's training camp in La Manga, south-eastern Spain. Hoddle made chopping the unfortunate half-dozen into a huge drama, which Beckham was not alone in finding 'ridiculous'.

United's survivors were Beckham, Gary Neville, Paul Scholes and Teddy Sheringham; all of them were particularly upset for two club mates who missed out in Phil Neville – distraught, as he had been told earlier by Hoddle's assistant John Gorman that he would be in – and Nicky Butt, but for the rest of the squad, and indeed the wider football world, the real story was the omission of Paul Gascoigne, who proceeded to trash Hoddle's room.

The draw, with an ageing Romania as the seeded team, plus Colombia and Tunisia, was regarded as favourable for an England squad that had reached the semi-final of Euro 96, lost only three games out of twenty under Hoddle and been reinvigorated by youngsters like Beckham and Scholes (both twenty-three) and the teenaged Owen, who had become England's youngest ever scorer at eighteen years and 164 days.

There was a shock awaiting Beckham, however, when the team to start the opening game against Tunisia in Marseille was read out to the players two days beforehand: Darren Anderton was in instead of him. 'It felt like somebody had hit me in the stomach,' was his reaction. Worse, he was immediately named among the players who would face the media that afternoon, answering questions about the forthcoming game, but having been told to pretend that the team had not been named.

Normally genial in front of the microphones and cameras, Beckham was so flat that other players started receiving calls asking what the matter with him was. Hoddle said in a brief and largely one-way conversation with him that he was 'not focused' and 'wrapped up in his own problems', which was taken to be a reference to Victoria (by now his fiancée).

Later the England manager would say his form had dropped off towards end of the season, and Tottenham's Anderton was better defensively in the favoured wing-back formation. 'It really jolted him as I knew it would,' Hoddle said. It certainly jolted Ted Beckham, whose reaction on taking his son's phone call about a supposed lack of focus was, 'I couldn't believe it. I've never heard so much rubbish in my life.'

England managers down the years have fought a constant battle to keep their team news secret, but once players know the starting XI and tell their relatives and agents, it is difficult to do so. The press inevitably picked up the rumours and some were not happy: 'How can the England manager jettison Beckham at this vital stage?' asked Steven Howard in the country's biggest selling daily, *The Sun*.

In *The Independent*, World Cup winner Jack Charlton, the Ireland manager, said, 'My choice would be to play Beckham wide on the right. There is no better crosser of the ball,' (which was true) 'and he goes past defenders more than Anderton does' (which was not).

Many papers had also been pushing in vain for Owen to start, so it was just as well for Hoddle that the game against Tunisia, the outsiders in the group, proved comfortable for England with a goal at the end of each half from Shearer and then Scholes. There was probably more incident in the clash between the respective sets of supporters on a nearby beach, where a giant screen was showing the match. Seats were used as missiles and two people were stabbed.

Owen was given 5 minutes as a late substitute, a miserable Beckham none, but the latter's chance would come in the second game against Romania.

After a difficult first half-hour for England in which Constantin Galca hit Seaman's crossbar, Paul Ince went down injured, so Beckham was summoned to play in the centre of midfield with David Batty.

He did well, Hoddle agreed, but Romania, inspired by veteran Gheorghe Hagi, were the better side and despite Owen eventually coming on to equalise Viorel Moldovan's goal with 11 minutes to play, there was a stunning blow for England in the final minute.

Graeme Le Saux was caught out as Dan Petrescu, a Chelsea colleague of his (and formerly of Hoddle's), jubilantly scored the winning goal.

Media representatives were predictably critical this time – all the more so when they discovered they had once again been misled at the manager's instigation by Gareth Southgate having to lie about his fitness.

Alex Ferguson used the *Sunday Times* column he was writing during the World Cup to criticise Hoddle and the FA for putting Beckham in front of the media so soon after the disappointment of being left out against Tunisia. Cheered up by his club manager and taken out of himself when readily agreeing to chat on the phone to a young English boy seriously ill in hospital, Beckham was at last given his chance when the side to play Colombia in the crucial third match was named: the winners would qualify and losers go home.

Colombia: Mondragon, Cabrera, Bermudez, Palacios, Moreno, Rincon, Serna (Aristazabal, 46), Lozano, Valderrama, Preciado (Valencia, 46), De Avila (Ricard, 46).
England: Seaman, G. Neville, Campbell, Adams, Anderton (Lee, 79), Beckham, Ince (Batty, 82), Scholes (McManaman, 73), Le Saux, Owen, Shearer.
Attendance: 41,275.

On the afternoon before the game, there was an insight into Beckham's mentality when he took a couple of bags of footballs out onto the training pitch on his own and spent two hours in the fierce heat hitting free-kicks at an empty goal. He might have been back in Chase Lane Park in Chingford, a little lad dreaming of playing for England, and learning that the harder you practise ...

In the 29th minute, England, already leading through Anderton's goal, won a free-kick almost 30 yards out in a central position. Beckham put the ball down and curled it perfectly over the yellow-shirted wall and into the net. He had scored his first England goal, as well as fulfilling his mother Sandra's request to mark her birthday with one. The temptation, he said some years later, was to run to Hoddle and gloat, which he resisted.

Even before the first goal, Scholes, Owen and Le Saux (from Beckham's cross) had all had chances to score and later defenders Sol Campbell and Adams, plus Shearer, Scholes and Owen could all have added to the margin against neat but toothless opposition. Colombia had been so demoralised by half-time that they sent on their full quota of three substitutes, to no great effect. Later the match would be immortalised in Kirsty MacColl's song about a bad date, 'England 2 Colombia 0' ('And I know just how those Colombians feel').

Sections of the press felt as vindicated as Beckham. In *The Sun*, Brian Woolnough awarded him nine out of ten, the joint top mark with Owen, and wrote, 'A truly magnificent goal and a free-kick that could transform his career. He must now stay in the side.'

By the end, as Beckham swapped shirts with Colombia's star player, Carlos Valderrama, England's only regrets were not having scored more goals, which hardly mattered, and finishing only second in the group, which did. It meant they would play the winners of Group H, Argentina, instead of the runners-up Croatia, with all the baggage that such a meeting entailed: 1966 and Sir Alf Ramsey's 'animals' jibe; 1986 and Diego Maradona's hand of God, and the Falklands War in between.

18

Argentina 2 England 2
(Argentina won 4-3 on Penalties)
World Cup Second Round (Saint-Etienne)
30 June 1998

It was 'the worst day of my life' and would leave him claiming to be 'the most hated man in England'. With the benefit of hindsight, others felt that events in Saint-Etienne that humid summer night would be the making of David Beckham.

After the desperate disappointment of playing for less than an hour of the opening two group games and consequent worsening of relations with Glenn Hoddle, Beckham felt he had made his point with the free-kick that effectively secured victory over Colombia and qualification for the knockout stage.

The second round match would prove one of England's most exciting at any World Cup. Newspapers hardly needed to stoke up the interest; *The Mirror,* which had had to apologise for its 'Achtung! Surrender!' headline before the Euro 96 semi-final against Germany, settled for '8pm tonight. It's payback time'.

England: Seaman, Neville, Adams, Campbell, Anderton (Batty, 96), Beckham, Ince, Le Saux (Southgate, 70), Scholes (Merson, 78), Owen, Shearer
Argentina: Roa, Vivas, Ayala, Chamot, Zanetti, Almeyda, Simeone (Berti, 91), Ortega, Veron, Batistuta (Crespo, 68), Lopez (Gallardo, 68)
Attendance: 30,600.

The game would be watched by up to twenty-six million people in the United Kingdom, one of ITV's top ten biggest audiences ever for any type of programme. Any viewers returning home late from work would have missed the earliest drama when England's goalkeeper David Seaman bowled over the Argentinian captain Diego Simeone, and Gabriel Batistuta scored from the penalty. Only 4 minutes later there was a softer one given at the other end after Michael Owen, wiser than his eighteen years, ran across the defender Roberto Ayala and went down, Alan Shearer converting his spot-kick with a confidence that belied the nature of the occasion.

With little more than quarter of an hour played, it was 2-1 from one of the goals of the tournament – one that made Owen's reputation. Taking Beckham's pass with a glorious touch he evaded one defender, veered past another, ignored the well-placed and more senior Paul Scholes, who was calling for the ball, and drove it past goalkeeper Carlos Roa.

Argentina had not previously conceded a goal for eight games, yet England had put two past them in the space of 6 minutes. There should have been another too: Scholes missed a good chance from 8 yards and was then at fault just before the end of a breathless first half when failing to pick up Javier Zanetti, who ran wide of England's defensive wall to equalise in a rehearsed free-kick move.

The experienced Diego Simeone, schooled in Spanish and Italian football and with more than seventy caps to his name, was, according to Beckham, an irritating opponent who would niggle away by fair means or foul and hope to provoke a reaction, which is exactly what he did, to catastrophic effect for England, just after half-time.

Beckham recalled being clattered from behind by the Argentinian captain, who then ruffled his hair and gave it a tug. Lying face down, he instinctively shot out a leg, catching Simeone just behind the knee and prompting him to crash theatrically to the ground. It was just what Simeone wanted, as he admitted some four years later.

Gary Neville was first to reach Beckham and asked 'What have you done?' But both knew. After showing Simeone a yellow card for the foul, the Danish referee Kim Milton Nielsen was suddenly showing a red one to Beckham, who half untucked his white shirt and walked away with a glazed look, glancing back once as if to check that this was really happening. There was no glance from Hoddle, who had immediately deputed one of England's masseurs, Terry Byrne, to take Beckham to the dressing room and was concentrating on reorganising his stunned troops.

In all, they would end up playing a man short for an hour and a quarter, and yet demonstrated such spirit and ability that they could still have won. Hoddle used Owen and Shearer cleverly, alternating them between wide midfield and attack to conserve energy, and was pleasantly surprised that Argentina did not push forward more. Not until extra-time did England feel it necessary to make a defensive substitution, fatefully bringing on David Batty for Darren Anderton.

Down in the dressing rooms, Beckham was in the shower when Steve Slattery, another masseur, rushed in and said Sol Campbell had scored, then rushed back to announce it had been disallowed (Shearer was adjudged to have put his arm across the goalkeeper Roa – another marginal decision). During the extra-time period when any 'golden goal' would have won the game, England were denied a penalty despite Jose Chamot handling the ball above his head under challenge from Shearer.

Nielsen subsequently maintained that all his major decisions were correct, saying of the red card, 'It was straightforward. The rules are very clear about kicking or attempting to kick an opponent.'

In the penalty shootout Argentina were the first to miss, but Paul Ince immediately had his shot saved. Shearer, Owen and Paul Merson scored but Batty, needing to do the same with what turned out absurdly to be the first penalty of his senior career, hit his shot too straight and Roa saved to send his team through to a quarter-final against Holland (which they would lose 2-1).

After watching some of the game on television in the drug testing room, Beckham was allowed to stand in the tunnel for extra-time and penalties, his mind all over the place. Afterwards he slumped onto a bench in the changing room next to Shearer. He appreciated Tony Adams coming over to offer condolences, but was aware that Hoddle had nothing to say to him, so asked John Gorman to offer the manager his apologies. A direct conversation did not happen until they were on the plane back to England the following day, when the manager, trying hard not to go into 'told you so' mode, said it was simply something he would have to learn from.

Newspaper coverage the following morning was summed up by *The Mirror*'s front-page headline: '10 Heroic Lions One Stupid Boy'. Later the paper ran a dartboard with Beckham's face on, so fans could 'get that fury out of your system ... hurl away until you eventually feel sorry for him. Be warned, it could take several hours.' Beckham, who was banned by FIFA for the next two competitive England matches and fined £2,000, issued a statement: 'This is without doubt the worst moment of my career. I will always regret my actions during last night's game.'

The ever loyal Neville wrote in his autobiography some years later – before starting work as one of Roy Hodgson's England coaches – that England and the FA 'chuck you overboard and look after their own. So Becks took all the flak.'

After escaping to New York to see Victoria, who was on tour with the Spice Girls, he returned to face more of that flak, which included seeing a picture of his effigy hanging from a lamp post outside the inappropriately named Pleasant Pheasant pub in South Norwood. Another publicity seeking London pub owner tried to sue him for decline in takings caused by England's exit

The best consolation Ted Beckham could draw from it all was that his son had 'become a man ... he had to'. A second one was to improve temporarily the relationship with Ferguson, who had rung him in New York. The Manchester United family, the message went, would look after him, which proved to be the case.

England squad member Rob Lee agrees, suggesting, 'In the end it taught him a fantastic lesson because a lot of people were against him, there was a lot of criticism. He came out of that very well, showed great strength of character to go through what he did at a young age and come through it.'

Hoddle, in his controversial diary of the tournament, maintained 'what happened against Argentina vindicated my judgment ... there's no way he'd even have thought of doing what he did against Argentina if his mind had been 100 per cent focused.' The events in France, he concluded, 'may leave a deep scar' and could even lead to Beckham being driven away from English football.

That was still five years away. Within seven months of the Argentina game Hoddle was sacked and Kevin Keegan appointed England manager, initially for four games only. By that time too, in February 1999, a revived Beckham would be over the first serious setback of his career – 'maybe I'd been leading a charmed life until that summer' – and like Manchester United was on his way to greater heights than ever before.

19

Arsenal 1 Manchester United 2
FA Cup Semi-Final Replay (Villa Park)
14 April 1999

Worried about becoming a pariah after taking the blame for England's World Cup failure, David Beckham found the Manchester United 'family' supporting him as promised and responded so well that he was able to play a full part in their collective attempt at making football history eleven months later.

In the very first League game of the new season he cemented his relationship with United supporters by scoring a last-minute equaliser from a trademark free-kick after the team had been 2-0 down at home to Leicester. West Ham, where the locals were threatening all manner of mayhem, was hardly the ideal venue for a first away game, but Beckham escaped from his native East London with his life, United escaped with a goalless draw and the worst was over.

From there, aside from a 3-0 League defeat by Arsenal (who had beaten them by the same score in the far less important Charity Shield), the season became better and better.

Arsenal's domestic Double of 1998 meant that United were no longer the only English club to have performed the feat more than once. It also confirmed that pair as the dominant sides of the late nineties.

As the following season moved towards a climax, however, only one of them was in a position to achieve a unique Treble. While the London side, playing their Champions League games at Wembley, had failed to progress beyond the group stage, United had come through a tough section by remaining unbeaten against Bayern Munich, Barcelona and Brondby, then seen off Internazionale 3-1 on aggregate, when the much hyped re-match between Beckham and his Argentine nemesis Simeone came to nothing and ended with an exchange of shirts. Juventus were now waiting in the semi-final and in between the two legs there were to be two more semi-final matches, against Arsenal.

In February the teams drew their return League game at Old Trafford 1-1, and most neutrals would probably have been happy for their fourth and final meeting of the season to be in the FA Cup final.

Instead the semi-final draw threw them together and on the same day that Newcastle were beating Tottenham in extra-time in the other game, the old rivals played out a rather disappointing goalless draw that left Ferguson cursing the extra fixture and referee David Elleray in equal measure. United were convinced that he should never have given Dwight Yorke offside when Roy Keane netted following a cross by Ryan Giggs .

With the unwanted replay – the FA Cup's last ever in a semi-final – scheduled only three days later back at Villa Park, Ferguson shook up his starting XI by bringing in Phil Neville, Ole Gunnar Solskjaer, Teddy Sheringham and Jesper Blomqvist for Denis Irwin, Andy Cole, Yorke and Giggs. Arsenal replaced Nelson Vivas, who had been sent off in extra-time during the first game, with Emmanuel Petit who had been serving his own suspension, and Freddie Ljungberg came in for Marc Overmars.

Arsenal: Seaman, Dixon, Keown, Adams, Winterburn, Parlour (Kanu, 104), Vieira, Petit (Bould, 119), Ljungberg (Overmars, 62), Bergkamp, Anelka.
Manchester United: Schmeichel, G. Neville, Johnsen, Stam, P. Neville, Beckham, Butt, Keane, Blomqvist (Giggs, 61), Sheringham (Scholes, 76), Solskjaer (Yorke, 91).
Attendance: 30,223.

The crowd may have dropped by 9,000 since the Sunday game, but those who made the effort to attend saw a classic. Beckham sat in the dressing room before kick-off pondering the fact that while he while he regarded Villa Park as a lucky ground after his winning goal in the 1996 semi-final, he had never scored against Arsenal.

It took 17 minutes to put that right. Sheringham, apparently surrounded by Arsenal players, kept his composure and the ball before feeding it back to Beckham, who from 25 yards beat his England training partner David Seaman, curling the shot away from him in a classic strike.

In the second half the tide appeared to be turning Arsenal's way. First Dennis Bergkamp veered inside and hit a low shot that Peter Schmeichel might have saved had it not deflected heavily off Jaap Stam. Only a few minutes later, with the yellow cards mounting up, as they often did between these sides (Beckham was one of four recipients in 7 minutes), Keane brought down Overmars to collect his second one and United were reduced to ten men.

The elegant Bergkamp has always been an Arsenal hero, but in the last minute of normal time came probably his worst moment in their shirt. Phil Neville's tired trip on Ray Parlour left the Dutchman standing over a penalty kick that could not only take his side back to Wembley, where he had missed the previous season's final because of injury, but would surely tilt the mental balance of the championship race as well as destroying United's Treble ambitions.

Bergkamp had missed three of his five previous penalties – the most recent one only a week earlier against Blackburn. No wonder he looked tense. This one was not his worst but Schmeichel guessed its direction and sprang to his left to save.

If that was Bergkamp's most horrible Arsenal memory, what followed in the second period of extra-time might just have been Patrick Vieira's. The French midfielder played a dreadful square pass just inside United's half to substitute Giggs, who set off on his way to one of the great FA Cup goals. Vieira managed to catch him but without winning back the ball, which seemed as the old cliché has it, to be glued to his feet as he next darted between Lee Dixon and Martin Keown, and shot high into the Holte End net as Tony Adams lunged in on him.

The celebration, with his white shirt whipped off a hairy chest and whirled round his head, was as memorable an image as the goal itself. Beckham found himself celebrating with fans who had spilled onto the pitch and who then at the final whistle lifted him onto their shoulders while trying to remove his shirt and boots.

Arsenal's manager, Arsene Wenger, with a second successive Double no longer possible, said,'It is not easy to take a defeat such as this. The two teams are very close to each other, it was a smashing game and in the end the luckiest won.'

Ferguson, who had already had a few verbal spats with his opposite number in their two-and-a-half year rivalry and would have many more, was naturally not having that. His verdict: 'Over the two legs I think we were the better team. The players have played in agony to get the victory. There's a lot of pain in there.'

Beckham rated it as good a game as he had ever played in and Gary Neville made it the best of his own 700-match career, claiming in retrospect that his team's momentum was now unstoppable. Which was just as well, given that Arsenal showed such formidable mental strength in winning their following two League games 5-1 and 6-1 while United faced a huge task next in Turin.

20

Juventus 2 Manchester United 3
(Aggregate 3-4)
Champions League Semi-Final Second Leg
(Turin)
21 April 1999

Scoring twice in the first 10 minutes of a game can never be regarded as a fault in a football team, unless they pay insufficient attention to what happens next.

That was the mistake Juventus made in the Stadio delle Alpi, although it still took an extraordinary effort from Manchester United to capitalise on it.

Given the levels of excitement reached on successive Wednesdays in Birmingham and Turin, it was just as well that the Saturday match in between them turned out to be a straightforward victory. Yet even then the stakes were high. United went into their first League game for a fortnight a point ahead of Arsenal and extended the lead for twenty-four hours by dismissing Sheffield Wednesday 3-0.

Beckham was one of those given a rest ahead of the second leg against Juventus, having been used as an example by Ferguson of the rotation policy implemented all season:

> People still occasionally criticise me for making changes and resting players but I think now is the time you will see its value. David Beckham is a case in point. He had a three-week break around Christmas, along with Paul Scholes and Gary Neville, and I think he has come to a peak at just the right time. His game has come together again as we saw with those marvellous crosses for Dwight Yorke's goals against Inter.

In the same press conference, Ferguson described Beckham as 'the best crosser of a ball in Europe', but there would be no praise after the home leg of the Juventus semi-final, despite his cross allowing Teddy Sheringham to flick the ball on for Ryan Giggs to score a late equaliser in a 1-1 draw. According to Roy Keane, there were some hard words spoken afterwards, notably for Giggs and Beckham for not working hard enough to win the ball back.

An ankle injury sustained late in the epic Arsenal replay and barely noticed at the time, meant Giggs was unavailable in Turin, giving a chance to Jesper Blomqvist, who would replace him until the last four games of the season.

Juventus: Peruzzi, Birindelli (Montero, 46), Iuliano, Ferrara, Pessotto, Conte, Deschamps, Davids, Di Livio (Fonseca, 80), Zidane, Inzaghi
Manchester United: Schmeichel, G. Neville, Johnsen, Stam, Irwin, Beckham, Butt, Keane, Blomqvist (Scholes, 68), Cole, Yorke
Attendance: 65,500

Already boosted by their away goal from Old Trafford, the Italians went ahead in only the 7th minute, when Inzaghi was left free on the far post to score, for which Neville accepted the blame. Soon afterwards the same player put his team 3-1 up on aggregate with a shot that went in off Jaap Stam's foot. 'Manchester United need a minor miracle,' television commentator Clive Tyldesley told the audience at home.

It was a time for footballing maturity rather than simple despair. Keane, who would go on to become the night's dominant figure, felt the match had become 'a mind game', a test of mental strength. The factors in United's favour, thin as they might have seemed, were that 80 minutes remained and that they knew Juventus' natural inclination would be to revert to Italianate caution, content to hold onto what they had. The response was admirable.

Soon Beckham was telling Neville with clenched fist 'we can do this'. Keane felt that one goal would put a little doubt in Italian minds and scored it himself with a fine header from Beckham's corner. The Irishman barely celebrated, turning and heading straight back to the halfway line.

Within a few minutes, he caught the World Player of the Year, Zinedine Zidane, a little late for a booking that would rule him out of the final if United were to make it. Unlike Paul Gascoigne in similar circumstances at the 1990 World Cup, however, Keane simply ploughed on, giving an individual performance that Ferguson said later it was 'an honour' to be associated with.

By half-time, when Yorke's diving header had equalised on the night, putting United in a winning position on away goals, the manager felt 'thoroughly relaxed'. Having seen what effect relaxation had on Juventus, he was not going to allow that sentiment to be transmitted to his players, bawling at the defenders as they sat in the dressing room to 'sort yourselves out'.

They continued to do so in the second half, during which United hit the woodwork twice and Peter Schmeichel was called into serious action only once, denying Inzaghi a hat-trick. Scholes, replacing Blomqvist, was soon booked for one of his infamous mistimed tackles and would also miss the final in Barcelona, which was confirmed as a reality when Cole scored the third goal as the ball rolled loose after goalkeeper Peruzzi had downed Yorke.

It only dawned on Keane at that point that 'there would be a final to miss'. Proud of the team and of his own contribution, he put his personal disappointment aside for a while, resolving to channel it into the chase for two other trophies. His take on Turin was that 'sometimes even Manchester United need the kind of confirmation that comes from a victory like this'.

Stam revealed some time later that his fellow Dutchman, Edgar Davids, the Juventus midfielder popularly known as 'Pitbull', had chased Beckham down the tunnel and abused him:

> I guess the whole situation took Becks by surprise because he didn't react. I think that was the start of his newfound maturity, which developed over that season. It seemed like the whole nation was on his back after he was sent off for kicking out at Diego Simeone in the World Cup.

For Beckham, who had become a father for the first time when Brooklyn was born in between the two Inter matches, Saint-Etienne was slowly being forgotten, and this was becoming a glorious period, albeit one in which so much could still go wrong. 'It felt like luck was starting to run our way when we needed it' was his summing up.

21

Manchester United 2 Newcastle United 0
FA Cup Final (Wembley)
22 May 1999

There was little time to rest and less to train in the month of May, during which Manchester United played seven of the most important games in the club's history, with David Beckham appearing in every minute of them.

If Sheffield Wednesday at Old Trafford without him had proved a comfortable fixture just before the trip to Turin, visiting Leeds United four days after the triumphant return from Italy was never going to fall into the same category. The previous day, Arsenal's thumping 6-1 win at Middlesbrough took them to the top of the table, where they stayed when United could only draw 1-1 at Elland Road.

With two games to play, the pair were level on points and goal difference, whereupon Leeds did United a huge favour for once by beating Arsenal the day before Alex Ferguson's side drew at Blackburn. All of which meant United would be champions if they won at home to Tottenham on the final day – 16 May.

Any suspicion that Spurs, sitting in mid-table, would rather surrender than help their North London neighbours to the title, were dispelled when they took the lead with Les Ferdinand's goal midway through the first half. Beckham, having missed one good chance early on, intervened by equalising with a characteristic whipped shot at a crucial time just before the interval.

Ferguson still carried out his plan to replace a disgruntled Sheringham at half-time with Cole, who justified the decision within a couple of minutes by scoring what turned out to be the winning goal.

According to Beckham, nobody sitting in the dressing room or in the long night of celebrations at the Marriott hotel was actually mentioning the T-word, but everybody was thinking it. One down, two cup finals in the space of four days to go.

Manchester United: Schmeichel, G Neville, My, Johnsen, P. Neville, Beckham, Keane (Sheringham, 9), Scholes (Stam, 78), Giggs, Cole (Yorke, 60), Solskjaer
Newcastle United: Harper, Griffin, Dabizas, Charvet, Domi, Lee, Hamann (Ferguson, 46), Speed, Solano (Maric, 68), Shearer, Ketsbaia (Glass, 79)
Attendance: 79,101.

Unbeaten in thirty-one games since a home loss to Middlesbrough in December, United were understandably strong favourites to complete the domestic Double. Newcastle, thirteenth in the Premiership for the second season in a row, had forced a goalless draw at Old Trafford in November, but lost the return 2-1 when Andy Cole scored twice against his former club. They had Alan Shearer, who had once badly disappointed Ferguson by not joining United from Southampton, but he had scored only eight goals in open play from thirty League appearances that season.

The only question in most minds was how strongly the forthcoming encounter against Bayern Munich would weigh on Manchester minds. It clearly had to influence Ferguson's team selection, even though several decisions were made for him: Keane and Scholes, being suspended for the Champions League tie, would both play; Denis Irwin, suspended after a controversial sending off at Liverpool, could not, so Phil Neville came in at left-back; Stam and Yorke were initially kept in reserve; and Nicky Butt was held back altogether. Beckham, asked if he wanted a rest after suffering from a mild virus, was alarmed by the very idea and responded with a predictable 'no chance, boss'.

Less predictable was an annoying change that had to be made in only the 9th minute of the final. Keane, caught by Gary Speed's tackle, tried to continue but had to come off. Once again Ferguson got the substitution right, turning to a man with something to prove in Sheringham, who within a couple of minutes of arriving finished off a smart passing move instigated by Cole and Scholes to give United the lead. Neither his own part in making the run into space before shooting, nor the weight of Scholes's pass could be underestimated.

There was little danger of retaliation from Newcastle, once again letting their supporters down in a Wembley final. As part of the enforced change, Solskjaer moved out wide on the right, allowing Beckham to switch to a more central role, where he played an important part in keeping up the high tempo that the manager had demanded despite the hot afternoon on a sluggish pitch. His 'tremendous' performance there, despite for once missing out on the assists, also convinced Ferguson that he could do the same job in that position against Bayern.

By half-time, Solskjaer, Cole and Sheringham could all have scored again, Schmeichel needing to make only one save, from the former Bayern man Didi Hamann.

Gullit tried to liven up Newcastle, facing a second successive FA Cup final defeat, by adding the physical presence of centre forward Duncan Ferguson to the mix, but with less than 10 minutes of the second half played, Sheringham and Scholes again conjured up a goal. Solskjaer intercepted a clearance down the line by Nikos Dabizas and fed Sheringham for a perfect lay-off to Scholes and an emphatic finish.

Before the end, with the result no longer in any doubt, Ferguson was able to bring on Stam and Yorke, giving them just enough game time to stay fresh without risking weariness, while ensuring there was no danger of injury to Cole, who was also pencilled in to start four days later. Thanks to the decision to play Beckham inside, there would be a place too for Blomqvist, who was able to remain seated in the Wembley sunshine throughout.

Gary Neville called the Wembley game the easiest of the run-in to the Treble, which was probably just as well. If the final itself was a little anticlimactic, the continuing Treble narrative kept the media happy.

The Observer headline was 'Triple double, treble chance', under which Ian Ridley made the point that with a European final only days away, United's unprecedented third Double in six seasons was in danger of being obscured:

> Once it was said that the Double couldn't be done, now it is becoming commonplace. Indeed, its significance has been almost forgotten amid Manchester United's assault on that Treble which has so far eluded an English club. It took them ninety-four years to achieve the old league and cup one-two; now they have done so three times in five years to surpass all rivals, such has been their domination of the domestic game this decade. It took any club sixty-one years. In the modern era, Tottenham's achievement was seen as beyond all, given the demands of the league's slog and the FA Cup's vagaries. It took Arsenal ten years to match it, Liverpool another fifteen.

Gullit lamented, without any great conviction,

> At some times we had the game in our hands and then we made a mistake and we were punished, but the big difference between them and us is that they have so much quality, especially in their movement, they can almost decide which time they can score a goal.

Ferguson, always on the lookout for a psychological advantage, even found a bonus in Keane's early injury: 'Everyone was saying that going to Barcelona without Roy Keane was a huge hurdle. Not anymore because Beckham in that role today was absolutely magnificent.'

Therein lay a significant clue to his strategy for the third and most dramatic leg of the Treble.

22

Bayern Munich 1 Manchester United 2
Champions League Final (Barcelona)
26 May 1999

In 1977 Liverpool went to the FA Cup final as League champions and with a European Cup final awaiting them, but managed to lose the middle game to Manchester United. Denying them the possibility of a Treble that year meant that twenty-two years later, United were in a position to become the first English side to complete one. In doing so they would also, of course, emulate Sir Matt Busby's 1968 side as European champions. The prospect encouraged 200 countries to take live television coverage.

Perhaps in retrospect a little too much was taken for granted. Completing the Double had been so straightforward that United were considered to be on an unstoppable roll. It appeared to have gone unnoticed that Bayern Munich, who they had been unable to beat in two Champions League group meetings that season, had just won the *Bundesliga* by 15 points, losing four games out of thirty-four, and were also in their domestic Cup final – therefore just like United in chasing a Treble that only Celtic (1967), Ajax (1972) and PSV Eindhoven (1988) had ever performed in their respective countries.

The prevailing attitude was summed up by Mark Hughes, possibly considered neutral on the basis of having played for both clubs as well as the hosts Barcelona: 'When you talk about Bayern nobody springs to mind that you are really frightened of but I'm sure when they think of the United team they can reel off five or six names to be very worried about.'

Beckham's new status was reflected in being allowed to choose the club suits – Versace, in grey with a prominent club badge – as well as being put forward for the main pre-match press interview. Quizzed about the essentials of his game, he came over well as a combination of devoted sportsman and cheeky chappie:

From seven or eight I could hit a ball quite a long way. What I've learnt since then is technique. I stay out for an hour hitting balls if the manager lets me. Sometimes when he sends me in I have tried to sneak back out but the manager's office has a view of everything so I can't get away with it.

With Keane and Scholes missing from his midfield quartet, Ferguson's biggest decision was how to compose that most important section of the team. In spite of the strong hint that the manager had dropped at Wembley, some papers still tipped Beckham to play wide, with Ronny Johnsen and Butt inside.

The Times, which had Gary Neville as a columnist, was able to forecast the strategy more accurately under the headline 'Ferguson puts his shirt on Beckham'. The back page revealed that the manager, who had overseen training symbolically wearing a (rather tight) red and white 1960s United shirt, would use his England midfielder centrally, with Giggs and Blomqvist on the flanks. As the paper pointed out,

> it heaps immense pressure on Beckham, of course, and shows just how much store Ferguson sets by the player who has been his most consistent performer this season. It throws him back into the heart of the side, back into the position in which he was playing when sent off for England against Argentina in the World Cup. A year on, Beckham, who was at the centre of a minor scare after training last night when an ice pack was strapped to his thigh as a precaution, is much better equipped to deal with the responsibility that has been heaped on his shoulders.

The scare did, indeed, prove minor, and before the kick-off Victoria Beckham, now the mother of two-month-old Brooklyn, and seated in the stand between her in-laws Ted and Sandra, was able to gaze down adoringly at her husband posing for a team photograph in which the happy-go-lucky Dwight Yorke was the only person smiling.

Bayern Munich: Kahn, Linke Matthuas (Fink, 79), Kuffour, Babbel, Jeremies, Effenberg, Basler (Salihamidzic, 89), Tarnat, Jancker, Zickler (Scholl, 70).
Manchester United: Schmeichel, G. Neville, Johnsen, Stam , Irwin, Giggs, Beckham, Butt, Blomqvist (Sheringham, 67), Cole (Solskjaer, 81), Yorke.
Attendance: 90,000

Once Pierluigi Collina set the game in motion, it was clear United had little to smile about. In fact, Ferguson later described Yorke as looking more nervous than he had ever seen him, and he was probably not the only one as Bayern made the early play and scored an early goal.

Jens Jeremies and Michael Tarnat split the defence and forced Johnsen into a foul on Carsten Jancker. As Mario Basler took the free-kick, Markus Babbel dragged Butt out of the wall, and the ball shot past Schmeichel.

The English champions, according to one report, looked 'frozen with tension' and, as Beckham admitted, they could hardly complain at being behind by the interval. Although the strategy he had devised was not working, Ferguson declined to make any changes, attempting to inspire the players with the message 'don't walk past the trophy at the final whistle without being entitled to touch it'.

As his team pushed forward after half-time, with no Keane to protect the back-four, they were vulnerable to counter-attacks. Jancker's backheel set up Christian Zickler, who dragged the chance wide, and Babbel glanced a header the wrong side of a post. The ineffectual Blomqvist scooped United's best chance over the bar from 6 yards and midway through the second half became the first man replaced, by Teddy Sheringham.

The game was in its last 10 minutes before Andy Cole, also poor on the night, made way for Ole Gunnar Solskjaer, at which point it should all have been too late. In the 74th minute Schmeichel had to make an excellent save from Stefan Effenberg, then Mehmet Scholl's chip floated over a helpless goalkeeper and hit the post, before Jancker's overhead kick came back off the bar.

Ferguson later admitted, 'I started to adjust to losing the game'. By the time Beckham placed the ball for a left-wing corner kick 25 seconds into added time, concerned that there was less room at the Nou Camp than many other grounds for his run-up, obituaries for a Treble had already been written. Any reporters who had pressed 'send' on their laptop were about to regret it amid what the next day's *Mirror* called 'the greatest two minutes in the history of sport'.

The sequence was officially timed at 120 seconds from the moment Beckham placed the ball for his first corner. Although right footed, from the left, it swung out rather than in, landing amid a crop of players including goalkeeper Schmeichel, playing his last game for the club, who had charged upfield. Yorke's header should have allowed Thorsten Fink to clear but his miskick landed at the feet of Giggs, whose attempted shot with his 'wrong' leg found Sheringham just onside and perfectly placed to turn it into the net.

Anyone who refuses to acknowledge the part fortune played in saving the game and the Treble should listen to Giggs: 'We were lucky the ball reached me, lucky I shanked it, lucky Teddy was there, lucky he scuffed it. But there's nothing wrong with being lucky.'

Coach Steve McClaren, an important influence since arriving at the club in January (his first game being an 8-1 away win at Nottingham Forest), immediately wanted to plan for extra-time, but Ferguson sensed Bayern were on their knees – in one or two cases, literally so. He waved his men back to the halfway line and then forward again and at 92 minutes and 10 seconds Solskjaer went down the left wing to win another corner.

Whether or not it was 'probably the best I ever took', Beckham's kick proved the most significant, Sheringham darting between two defenders to glance a header across goal for Solskjaer to hammer into the roof of the net. The final whistle followed within a minute, prompting exactly opposite scenes to those that had been imagined only a short time earlier.

Beckham raised enough of a gallop to run to the United end and celebrate in front of the club's supporters. Ferguson was grabbed by ITV's Gary Newbon and came out with one of the sport's most enduring soundbites: 'I can't believe it. Football, bloody hell!'

He has insisted ever since that United were the only team trying to attack (which of course they had to do after conceding in the 6th minute) and that his controversial team selection had worked well, with Beckham the best midfielder on the pitch, Effenberg anonymous and Giggs, he felt, giving left-back Tarnat a hard time.

Gary Neville, however, admitted many years later that it was only when Beckham and Giggs reverted to their normal positions that United started flowing and that the team shape had not worked well.

For the later editions of the newspapers, most reporters had time – though not much – to marry astonishment, admiration and sober judgment. Glenn Moore had a reasoned assessment in *The Independent*:

Beckham played well throughout, using the ball well and always available, but with the front pair anonymous, Giggs predictable and Blomqvist marginalised on the flanks, United had no attacking threat.

... United were fortunate last night but they deserve their success. They are unbeaten in 13 European ties, during which they have always sought to attack and scored 31 goals. The ghosts of '68 have been laid.

Richard Williams, in the same paper, wrote,

It was a victory achieved in the face of opponents convinced they had done enough to win. Bayern Munich's players will be asking themselves this morning whether they relaxed too much in the final stages or whether they were simply beaten by a team that does not know how to lose – and, in fact, has not lost a match of any kind since before Christmas

... Beckham's corner kicks, from both left and right, were United's only consistently dangerous tactic, and the least surprising thing about the match's denouement was that both goals came from that source.

In the end the biggest gamble of Ferguson's life paid off, ending a season in which he and his players really have made history, enthralling and astonishing the rest of us along the way.

Most writers spoke well of Beckham, especially Matt Dickinson, whose *Times* piece was headlined 'Beckham factor is difference between defeat and victory' and said,

David Beckham was given so many responsibilities last night that they might as well complete the set this lunchtime and ask him to pilot Concorde home. After this triumph of the human spirit, the boy from Leytonstone would probably shrug his shoulders, grab the joystick and take Manchester United on another flight of fantasy.

United's match winner may have been Ole Gunnar Solskjaer, but it was Beckham who ensured that his team approached the final mad minutes with an air of hope rather than resignation. Beckham has played better games but never has he displayed such indomitable will.

Emerging from the dressing room, the man himself told reporters, 'It's one of the best feelings in the world, especially with being 1-0 down with a minute to go. I've had a big year with the birth of my son, and that was the most special thing that could ever have happened to me, but this is next.'

Finding himself alone with the trophy later, he requested a club photographer to take his picture out on pitch with it, then met his dad in an embrace with both recalling the similar hug in Saint-Etienne eleven months earlier in circumstances about as different as could be.

Earlier that month Gary Neville had summed it up in a newspaper interview: 'The abuse he has had to put with has been terrible, what he has had to go through last summer was nothing short of scandalous in my opinion, but I knew it wouldn't crack him. He has had too good a schooling at this club for that to happen.'

History, it is said, is written by the winners, and in this case history was made by them.

Manchester United 2 Real Madrid 3
(Madrid won 3-2 on Aggregate)
Champions League Quarter-Final Second Leg
(Old Trafford)
19 April 2000

Football managers are generally all in favour of their players getting married, as a means of settling them down, preferably with the additional responsibility of becoming a parent as soon as possible. On the other hand, when the occasion becomes regarded as a coronation of the country's most famous celebrity couple (red velvet thrones and all), followed by a £150,000 Ferrari birthday present and a new house 200 miles away, the manager in question may wonder where it will all end.

The answer, within four years of David and Victoria tying the knot in Ireland on 4 July 1999, was in divorce – from the football club. In retrospect, the 1999–2000 season offered plenty of clues to that outcome.

As we have seen, the previous triumphant campaign ended with Alex Ferguson – who was knighted the following month – singing Beckham's praises. However, he had never been keen on the relationship with Victoria and from the time of the wedding, his generally affectionate paternal approach turned into something sterner.

David's first mistake was not only to request a couple of extra days for his honeymoon before returning to pre-season training, but to do it through his agent approaching the chairman, Martin Edwards. Ferguson was outraged, as the blast down the telephone made clear; Beckham ended up coming back earlier than United's other England players and training with the reserves.

In September he was fined £50,000 (two weeks' wages), for appearing at Jade Jagger's London Fashion week party the night before United flew to Austria for their Champions League game against Sturm Graz.

There was then a threat to kidnap his wife and child (see next Chapter), and a court case in which he successfully appealed against a speeding fine and ban, but had to deny making up a story about a man trying to grab his son outside Harrods.

Further controversies he was involved in during the season included a series of yellow cards, a stamping incident with Jamie Redknapp at Anfield, obscene abuse to Leeds supporters (who had offered plenty of their own) and a red card at the ill-fated World

Club Championship in Brazil in January, the timing of which competition meant United were unable to defend the FA Cup.

The following month brought a furious row with Ferguson after Beckham turned up late for training because Brooklyn had been ill. Deciding to make a stand and a point, Sir Alex sent Beckham to train with the reserves (which he refused to do) and dropped him for a key game away to main title challengers Leeds. United won it 1-0 to remain favourites.

A month later after clear-the-air-talks, *The Independent* was headlining 'Beckham and Sir Alex put differences aside', quoting the manager as saying 'the players know I don't hold grudges' while Beckham dismissed reports of a transfer to Arsenal, by saying,

> It annoyed me to read I am leaving Manchester United because there's no other club I want to play for. I couldn't see myself playing for another club in this country. It has never even crossed my mind. I've said in the past that at some stage I might want to play abroad. But at the moment all I can see ahead of me is turning out for United and helping them to be even more successful.

Competing for seven trophies meant there was every chance of that. Even after defeats in four of the least meaningful ones – the Charity Shield, European Super Cup, League Cup and World Club Cup – United had won the Inter Continental Championship against Palmeiras of Brazil and were going well in the two competitions that mattered most to them. Leeds, after closing to within 4 points in the Premiership, were falling away, and defence of the European crown had been smooth, with only two defeats in twelve games under the new system of two group stages.

All of which led to a quarter-final against Real Madrid, laden with historical echoes.

Manchester United: Van Der Gouw, G. Neville, Stam, Berg (Sheringham, 61), Irwin (Silvestre, 46), Beckham, Keane, Scholes, Giggs, Yorke, Cole (Solskjaer, 61).
Real Madrid: Casillas, Salgado, Karanka, Campo, Carlos, McManaman (Karembeu,89), Redondo, Helguera, Savio (Geremi,61), Raul, Morientes (Anelka,72)
Attendance: 59,178.

It was Real Madrid, on their way to five successive European Cup wins, who United went out to in the 1957 semi-final – the first and last that the original Busby Babes played in. In 1968 the Best-Charlton-Law team defeated the Spaniards 4-3 at the same stage en route to winning the competition for the first time. Now as defending champions, England's Treble winners were thrown up against a gifted side featuring home-grown heroes like teenage goalkeeper Iker Casillas and Raul, plus a couple of exotic South Americans in Roberto Carlos (Brazil) and Fernando Redondo (Argentina), with extra spice – or Spice Boy – in Steve McManaman – a beaten Liverpool player in the white suit FA Cup final of 1996.

Real, under Vicente del Bosque, had nevertheless finished only runners-up to Bayern Munich in their second group section, losing to them 4-2 and 4-1. United's players were happy to draw the first leg of the quarter-final 0-0 at the Bernabeu, although Ferguson wasn't, claiming goalkeeper Mark Bosnich saved them in what he called their worst performance in a big game for a long while.

League form was certainly offering every reason for confidence: wins by 4-0 and 7-1 over Bradford City and West Ham going into the away leg, then 4-3 and 4-0 against Middlesbrough and Sunderland before the home match, left them 11 points clear at the top with five games to play.

Another Premiership title was virtually assured and what remained was to become the first team to successfully defend the European Cup under its Champions League format. 'While I was unhappy with them in Madrid, we will play well this time,' Ferguson promised, adding, 'Giggs and Beckham have been fantastic this season and as a pair are playing better than they have ever done.'

All of which seemed a little over optimistic when United were 3-0 down after 53 minutes. From the start Madrid seemed to adopt the attitude that an away goal would put them in the driving seat, and Roberto Carlos was a particularly lively attacker down the left flank.

He even had a chance himself after quarter of an hour, but was thwarted by Raimond Van der Gouw, deputising for the injured Bosnich. Dwight Yorke put a header wide before, in the 20th minute, Madrid went ahead.

Referee Pierluigi Collina played advantage, allowing McManaman to feed a pass to Michel Soldado on the right. Roy Keane moved to intercept his cross at the near post, but managed only to slice it into his own net.

At the interval, by which time Casillas had saved from Beckham and Keane and Real had twice threatened again on the break, United had to replace the injured Denis Irwin. Content to keep the same formation, they brought on Mikael Silvestre, but within a couple of minutes were in desperate straits after conceding a second goal. McManaman led a swift break and found Raul, who cut inside Silvestre and easily beat Van der Gouw.

Almost before Ferguson could react with the necessary substitutions, a brilliant piece of skill by Redondo set up Raul for another goal and the tie was effectively over with more than half an hour to play. Teddy Sheringham and Ole Gunnar Solskjaer, the heroes of Barcelona, duly arrived, but with United needing four goals their task was almost impossibly difficult this time.

Beckham raised hopes in the 66th minute by wriggling past two defenders and scoring one of the best goals of a type not often seen from him.

Had one more effort, from Scholes or Solskjaer, gone in shortly afterwards, Madrid might have been lured into panic. Casillas was proving his worth, however, and only a few minutes remained when he was beaten again, from a penalty. McManaman conceded it, bringing down Keane, and Scholes scored.

It was United's first home defeat in sixteen months and even Ferguson was forced to admit 'you have to accept it, the best team won on the night'. McManaman, trying not to gloat, said 'Everyone expected us to get beaten, so it's nice to come here and turn the tables.'

'United's crown is torn from their heads' was the *Daily Mail* back page, the match report inside awarding the game a maximum five stars but reading,

> So gloriously won, so humiliatingly lost ... Ferguson's team may attack with verve and panache but all campaign they have looked vulnerable at the back. The manager's failure to find a defensive partner for Jaap Stam may not have prevented them cantering to another title, but against world-class strikers they were always likely to be found out.

It would have been fascinating for United to have met Bayern again in the semi-final. As it was, Real took handsome revenge for their two defeats by the Germans in the group matches, beating them 3-2 on aggregate and easily overcoming fellow Spaniards Valencia 3-0 in the final.

United's consolation was to seal the Premiership in their very next game, when Beckham put them on their way to victory at Southampton with the first goal. He scored again in the final home game against Spurs, after which Ferguson was reported to have 'anger in his voice' as he said in his traditional speech on the pitch,

> We had to travel halfway round the world to Tokyo and then face another long haul to Brazil for the World Club Championship. We did win it by a distance – and the reason for that is that we put people under pressure. Points are points and our rivals found it difficult to live with us. The pressure got to them and this season we produced it a bit earlier to get a huge and handsome winning margin. This is probably the best championship we have won. But I know the players will be in a bitter-sweet mood.

It had come to something when they were disappointed at 'only' winning the League by eighteen points. Any bitterness on Beckham's part was less concerned with the football, in which he had excelled again, more with his slowly deteriorating relationship with the manager.

24

England 2 Portugal 3
European Championship (Eindhoven)
12 June 2000

At the height of the tension with Ferguson, it had been during an international break for the goalless draw at home to Argentina that regular roommate Gary Neville persuaded Beckham to make his uneasy peace with the manager.

Apart from the mayhem of Saint-Etienne and its aftermath, playing for England was always a source of pride and pleasure to him, and once Kevin Keegan took over from Glenn Hoddle early in 1999 he was even more firmly established.

Beckham found Keegan, who was very much a players' man, 'brilliant', not least for the great sympathy he showed over two upsetting incidents involving the new Mrs Beckham during that season.

The first came the day before a home game against Luxembourg, when Victoria phoned to tell her husband about a threat to kidnap her and Brooklyn while the match was on. Keegan, who had experienced death threats to his own wife while playing for Hamburg twenty years earlier, insisted on Victoria and the baby joining them at the security-conscious team hotel and offered to leave David out of the next day's game and the vital one in Poland four days later.

Beckham was happy to play in both; the four points gained earned England a two-leg play-off against Scotland, which they came through despite a 1-0 home defeat.

Keegan was an admirer of Beckham's as a player and a person, suggesting 'he has no ego' (which would have surprised some of his critics). He was regarded as having an important role to play at the finals in Belgium and Holland, where England were given an awkward looking draw against Germany, Romania and Portugal.

On the eve of the opening game against the Portuguese, Alan Shearer did nothing to dispel the usual optimistic talk about winning the tournament. 'I'm not saying we are going to, but I firmly believe we can,' he said, adding that in David Beckham and Luis Figo the opposing teams had 'the best two crossers in the world'.

The Daily Telegraph reported that 'in training Beckham has been making the ball move like a swallow at play' and predicted 'England should get the result they need'.

Victoria, having been present for all the drama of the Bayern Munich final in Barcelona a year earlier, decided she and her father would travel to considerably less glamorous Eindhoven for the game, which was to prove unwise.

England: Seaman, G. Neville, Campbell, Adams (Keown,81), P. Neville, Beckham, Ince, Scholes, McManaman (Wise,57), Shearer, Owen (Heskey, 46).
Portugal: Vitor Baia, Xavier, Jorge Costa, Fernando Couto, Dimas, Paulo Bento, Vidigal, Figo, Rui Costa (Beto,85), Joao Pinto (Conceicao,76), Nuno Gomes (Capucho,90).
Attendance: 33,000.

The Beckhams and every other English fan could hardly have been happier after 18 minutes play, when two of David's crosses had brought goals. In only the 4th minute, Shearer on the left switched the play to him for a curled centre that United teammate Paul Scholes headed in.

Within quarter of an hour there was a second, from another fine Beckham assist, converted by McManaman, whom he was happy to have on the same side this time.

Perhaps complacency crept in. Portugal began to exploit greater numbers and authority in the centre of midfield, where Scholes and Ince were overrun and denied extra assistance.

'I was laughing on the bench when I saw England's defenders retreating to their penalty area rather than trying to tackle Figo or Rui Costa,' Portuguese substitute Paulo Sousa said later. He had plenty to laugh about as Adams stood off Figo, who pulled one goal back and Rui Costa's diving header beat David Seaman for the equaliser, all before half-time.

At the interval Keegan brought off Michael Owen, who never liked him and was left 'baffled and hurt'. McManaman joined him in the dressing room 12 minutes into the second half, but neither Emile Heskey nor Dennis Wise had much to offer as replacements, and just before the hour Nuno Gomes met Rui Costa's pass and lifted the ball over Seaman for the winning goal.

It was the first time since the 1970 World Cup quarter-final against West Germany that England had lost after holding a two-goal lead. *The Daily Telegraph* summed up:

England suffered the falsest of starts to their Euro 2000 campaign here last night, flying out of the blocks but soon tripping up in the teeth of the superior passing and tactics of Portugal, for whom Luis Figo and Rui Costa proved endless fonts of invention. Only David Beckham and Paul Scholes emerged from the wreckage of England's ambitions with reputations enhanced.

Keegan agreed with that assessment of Beckham's performance saying, 'he won't have put in a better performance in an England shirt', but a few fans seated behind the dug-out nevertheless found it necessary to scream abuse at Beckham before making tasteless remarks about his wife and adding 'I hope your baby gets cancer'.

Caught on camera responding to them with a middle finger, he found himself pictured on the front pages, although it was another twenty-four hours before the real story emerged under headings like 'Beckham suffers torrent of invective' and 'Shining star sullied by abuse'. As Paul Hayward wrote in *The Telegraph*, 'The creator of both England goals against Portugal was the victim of vicious personal abuse from followers of his own team.'

Fortunately Keegan, who had been walking off right behind him and heard everything, was able to put the incident into context. That did not prevent one of those outraged *Daily Mail* headlines to which the answer is invariably 'no' asking of Beckham 'Is this man a national liability?'

At the next game against Germany, further blighted by outbreaks of hooliganism beforehand, decent England supporters chanted 'there's only one David Beckham', and there was better humour all round after he served up a free-kick for Shearer to score the only goal.

The mood soured again after the final match against Romania, however, when a 2-1 lead was transformed into a 3-2 defeat, meaning elimination along with the even more hapless Germans. Phil Neville's error led to the winning goal, and it was his turn to become a national scapegoat, arriving home to find graffiti on his garden wall. Like his brother, he would hear his name booed at future England games, while Beckham in contrast had found widespread sympathy and respect, with more to come.

25

Italy 1 England 0
Friendly (Turin)
15 November 2000

Of all the moments that had Ted Beckham bursting with even more pride than his son, David captaining England for the first time was right up there. The fact that the match was lost hardly mattered in the greater scheme of things.

The occasion was, if not a new era, then the bridging point from an old one. Immediately after a 1-0 home defeat by Germany a month earlier in the final match played before Wembley Stadium was given an overdue makeover, Kevin Keegan had told the players 'that's it lads, I've had enough' and resigned, despite attempts by Tony Adams, an emotional Beckham and Football Association officials to talk him out of it.

Howard Wilkinson, an FA stalwart, took charge for the goalless draw in Finland four days later, and although Sven-Goran Eriksson had been announced as new manager he was still needed by his Italian club, Lazio, and was merely an observer as Peter Taylor, Leicester City's manager, took charge for the friendly in Turin.

With Alan Shearer having retired from international football after Euro 2000, Adams had been named captain for the first two games of the new season, and then Martin Keown wore the armband when he was missing against Finland.

Sol Campbell would subsequently claim he would have been captain if he had been white, presumably thinking that post-Shearer was his time. Taylor decided the candidates were Gary Neville, Gareth Southgate and Beckham, and opted for the youngest of them to lead a youthful team selected against Italy, which of course increased the attention and celebrity value that Sir Alex Ferguson so disliked.

Within a month Beckham was named fifty-ninth most influential individual in the country, ahead of the Prince of Wales among others. An ITV documentary, *The David Beckham Story*, drew ten million viewers (and was criticised for lack of substance), although a first television interview with Michael Parkinson, who became an admirer, was better received.

'I'm surprised to find myself in this position because it was only two years ago I wasn't liked by a lot of people,' the new captain said without any obvious bitterness.

The amiable Taylor, previously England's Under-21 manager, was soon reminded about the reality of international football when Michael Owen and Paul Scholes dropped out the day before the game. That did not deflect him from reverting to the 3-5-2 formation favoured by his friend and former Spurs teammate Glenn Hoddle, with Beckham and Nicky Butt among the central midfield trio and Neville outside them as right wing-back.

For United's contingent, it was a return to Juventus' Stadio delle Alpi nineteen months after the dramatic Champions League semi-final, albeit with only 22,000 present this time on a wet November night.

Italy: Buffon, Cannavaro, Nesta (Adani, 67), Maldini (Bertotto, 74), Di Livio (D. Zenoni, 52), Albertini (Di Biagio, 52), Gattuso, Coco, Fiore, F. Inzaghi (Del Piero, 73), Delvecchio (S. Inzaghi, 61).
England: James, Ferdinand, Southgate, Barry (Johnson, 73), G. Neville, Beckham, Butt (Carragher, 25), Dyer (Fowler, 83), Parlour (Anderton, 78), Barmby, Heskey (Phillips, 73). **Attendance:** 22,000

In contrast to England's experiments, Italy, under Giovanni Trapattoni, fielded a strong, experienced side that nevertheless had things far from their own way. Butt was forced off with an injury after only 25 minutes, giving Jamie Carragher his second cap as the enforcer alongside Beckham, who produced one of his team's first efforts with a drive from 30 yards that Gianluigi Buffon initially fumbled before recovering.

Although the second half was littered with almost a dozen substitutions, the game livened up, notably when Buffon saved from Ray Parlour. Beckham was brought down and Gennaro Gattuso, the combative former Rangers midfielder, appeared to give him a slap on the head. 'Gattuso tried to provoke him and there was a little tussle,' Taylor recalled many years later. 'What did David do? He walked away. I knew then my decision was right.'

Soon afterwards a classic Italian counter-attack caught the visitors out and Gattuso hammered a 30-yard drive past David James. It turned out to be the only goal, as Emile Heskey's strong appeal for a penalty was rejected, Buffon kept out Seth Johnson's first touch in international football and Southgate missed with a header from Beckham's corner.

In the circumstances it was regarded as a satisfactory performance: 'The way some of them performed tonight, they deserved to win,' Taylor said. Neville claimed that England had out-passed the Italians and offered a predictably positive endorsement of his friend and club mate as captain:

David has six or eight years of playing for England left and I am sure he will be a worthy captain for that time. He does not talk to people a lot naturally but sometimes one little word can mean more than five or six minutes from another player. A 'well done' from Eric Cantona would put me in the clouds and it is the same for David Beckham. That is all you need sometimes. You need a figurehead as England captain like Tony Adams, Alan Shearer and Bryan Robson, and David is the same.

The captain himself not surprisingly called it 'the proudest moment of my international career' and from that moment there seemed little debate about whether he should continue in the job, not least because Adams had followed Shearer into international retirement. Like many foreigners, Eriksson seemed less bothered than the British about who should be captain. He joked at the time that his fourteen-year-old daughter Lina, a Beckham admirer, had made the decision but some months later said,

> David Beckham behaved like a captain from the first. From day one with me, he was extremely good on the pitch. He's not the type to stand on the table to address the team, but you can see that he is concerned about everything that happens within the squad. He communicates with me and the rest of the staff like a captain and he's got better at it with experience.

Simon Barnes in *The Times* noted how the latest honour completed the transformation from the pariah of Saint-Etienne 1998 and offered credit where it was due:

> The transition in public opinion is a tribute to Beckham himself. He responded by having the season of his life. It was a personal triumph ... Still only 25, with growing authority, he could become something to wonder at as he moves towards his peak.

Arguably, that peak was barely a year away.

26

Manchester United 6 Arsenal 1
Premiership (Old Trafford)
25 February 2001

In David Beckham's 2003 autobiography, *My Side,* Manchester United's 2000–01 season is barely mentioned. Why would it be? After all, they only won the League by 10 points, completing a hat-trick of titles and beating their supposedly closest rivals 6-1 along the way, after one of the most extraordinary halves of football seen at Old Trafford during all his time there. United's supremacy was almost being taken for granted. From early in the season, some of the football had been stunning. Beckham, in a wide-ranging interview with *The Observer,* designed as part of a charm offensive before Andrew Morton's controversial biography about him and Victoria was published, said of the away game at Everton in September,

> The first half was probably the most enjoyable game of football I've played in, not because we were hammering them, or winning two or three-nil, but just the way we were playing. It was such good football, such enjoyable football, the way we were passing the ball about, the times I was getting on the ball.

The final score that day was 3-1 – all United's goals having come in the first half. Beckham, given a target of fifteen goals for the season by Sir Alex Ferguson, had earlier scored in three games in succession, including the 6-0 demolition of Bradford City. The Everton game confirmed them as League leaders – a position surrendered for only one match, after losing 1-0 to Arsenal at Highbury in the first week of October – which would make the return game four months later all the sweeter.

By that time they had lost only one other League match – annoyingly, at home to Liverpool – but were already thirteen points ahead of Arsene Wenger's side.

Manchester United: Barthez, G. Neville, Brown, Stam, Silvestre, Beckham, Butt, Keane (Chadwick, 75), Scholes, Yorke (Sheringham, 75), Solskjaer.

Arsenal: Seaman, Luzhny, Grimandi, Stepanovs, Cole (Ljungberg, 45), Pires, Vieira, Parlour (Vivas, 69), Silvinho, Wiltord, Henry.
Attendance: 67,535.

It was hardly the best day for Arsenal to be without Lee Dixon, Martin Keown and Tony Adams, stalwarts of the team's back-four, and in their absence the makeshift defence was simply overrun, even with Silvinho, a left-back, playing in midfield to protect the young Ashley Cole. In contrast, United did not miss either Ryan Giggs or Andy Cole, with Dwight Yorke coming back for a rare start and making hay with a hat-trick by half-time.

His first goal arrived within a couple of minutes, from a one-two with Scholes. The shock of the afternoon, in retrospect, was that Arsenal managed to equalise after quarter of an hour, through Thierry Henry, who had won the Highbury game with a spectacular volley. Once again he beat his compatriot Fabien Barthez, this time with a low shot at the near post.

Almost immediately Roy Keane hit a ball over the top of Arsenal's suspect central defence, and Yorke, played on by Gilles Grimandi, restored United's lead from just inside the penalty area.

The Latvian Igor Stepanovs simply could not cope, and midway through the first half Arsenal were 3-1 down after Beckham played a superb 40-yard crossfield pass beyond him that Yorke chested down before beating the increasingly exposed David Seaman.

It was 4-1 with less than half-an-hour played as Yorke beat Stepanovs again out on the left touchline and fed Keane, who scored from 10 yards out. From having managed only four goals in their previous six League and Cup games, United had scored that many in barely 25 minutes and remarkably there was another to come before a shell-shocked Arsenal could retreat to the dressing room: Nicky Butt left Grimandi on his backside and cut the ball back for Ole Gunnar Solskjaer to add the fifth.

Wenger was unusually and justifiably angry at half-time. He brought on Freddie Ljungberg for Cole, moving Silvinho to full-back, but did not even bother using Dennis Bergkamp, who had been surprisingly dropped. Arsenal presumably considered that the match and the championship were now far beyond them and would have been satisfied with a goalless second half, a hope ruined in the final minute when former Tottenham man Teddy Sheringham, having earlier headed wide from Beckham's free-kick, made it 6-1.

A bitterly disappointed Wenger said,

I have had worse experiences but the size of the score makes this a very bad one. Defensively we were too poor. Nobody was communicating, we had no leaders and there were times when we looked like a youth team. We are not into March yet and it hurts me that the title is already over. It is not good for the League and I am not proud of that.

Even 16 points clear, Ferguson refused to accept the title was decided, although he said,

> Arsenal are finished for the League now. This is a big blow for them. I will not say we
> have won the League because we have Liverpool and Leeds to play. If I start talking
> about the title being won the players might relax and I don't want that. They are better
> when they are on edge and they were on edge here.

It was an interesting insight into the psychology of his approach, but as *The Independent*
reported the next day, 'This was not so much a football match, more a coronation.
Sixteen-point leads do not disappear inside 10 matches, not even in the funniest of old
games.'

It did not, of course, but the rest of the season became something of an anticlimax,
summed up by losing the last three League games and by Ferguson's confirmation
that he would retire in a year's time. Already knocked out early in the League Cup (by
Sunderland) and the FA Cup (at home to West Ham), United were once again denied in
Europe when Bayern Munich extracted revenge for the 1999 defeat by beating them in
both legs of the Champions League quarter-final. That brought a typically forthright
denunciation from Keane, who went as far as to say,

> Maybe it is the end of the road for this team, I'm not sure. We were lucky to get through
> the first group stage even. Teams like Real [Madrid] seem to be going further ahead and
> we seem to be going further behind. It's time to bring in new faces. But that's not my
> department.

Beckham, pipped by Sheringham for both the PFA and Football Writers' Player of the
Year awards, was less pessimistic, having told *The Observer* earlier in the season:

> I don't think I'm at my peak yet and I don't think this team is at its peak yet. Because
> most of us are still young, still 25 and 26, we've still got a lot to learn from the game.
> There are still a lot of trophies to be won. We are not getting ahead of ourselves and
> we're not being big-headed.

27

Germany 1 England 5
World Cup Qualifying Group (Munich)
1 September 2001

Even though it was a difficult time for Manchester United, there is a sustainable argument that the 'peak' David Beckham and others spoke about him reaching occurred in the autumn of 2001. Given that two of the most famous England games of both men's career were played around that time, the same could be said of Sven-Goran Eriksson.

The previous season ended with Beckham scoring a late goal on 6 June to confirm England's 2-0 victory away to Greece in their World Cup qualifying group. It was an important success, but still left them 6 points behind Germany, who had played a game more – the group winners qualified automatically; the runners-up would go into a play-off.

After Keegan, the players, public and media appreciated the calm, studious approach employed by Eriksson, who had finally severed ties with Lazio to take over at the start of the year, and with the victory in Athens became the only England manager ever to win his first five matches.

That record was ended when Holland comfortably won a friendly at White Hart Lane in August, a result difficult to assess as the Swede changed almost the whole team at half-time. He had insisted throughout that England could win in Munich, a feeling that Beckham came to share, telephoning his good friend Dave Gardner back at home to tell him so.

His greater concern was a groin strain that had forced him off during United's last match, a 1-1 draw at Aston Villa, and according to some reports 'reduced him to tears'. For most of the week he trained on his own and could only join in on the day before the match, so that his fitness became one of many talking points in the intense media build-up.

The *Times* front page on the morning of the game highlighted another one in its main headline 'Hooligan invasion tests police', with dire warnings about potential trouble alongside a picture of Beckham during training. The captain's broad smile should have hinted at his availability, although in the sports section Matt Dickinson wrote,

The need for England to be at their best underlines the importance of having Beckham fit and while the captain came through training yesterday there is no assumption among the coaches that he will finish the game even if he does feel strong enough to start.

UEFA having decided to make the play-off draw the previous day, England now knew that they would probably face Belarus, rather than the more dangerous Holland or Portugal if they were to finish second, which would almost certainly be their fate unless they could pull off a first victory in Germany since 1965.

Germany: Kahn, Worns (Asamoah, 46), Nowotny, Linke, Rehmer, Hamann, Ballack (Klose,67), Bohme, Deisler, Jancker, Neuville (Kehl,78).
England: Seaman, G. Neville, Ferdinand, Campbell, A. Cole, Beckham, Gerrard, Scholes (Carragher,83), Barmby (McManaman,62), Heskey (Fowler, 53), Owen.
Attendance: 63,000.

'If we play well, and have some luck, we can win,' Eriksson had repeatedly told reporters. Nobody could have imagined how well his team could play (in the second half at least), or how well they would win.

Yet it is still easy to forget how difficult the game had been for England until the stroke of half-time. Germany were in front in only the 7th minute when Oliver Neuville nodded down and the big Bayern striker Carsten Jancker poked the ball past David Seaman.

Wearing a pair of tight lycra cycling shorts to help his groin, Beckham felt uncomfortable so immediately removed them and began to exert a crucial influence on the game with his set-pieces and long passes into the space left by Germany's wing-backs.

England quickly equalised, after his free-kick was not cleared and Nicky Barmby headed back to Michael Owen, but the home side should have regained the lead. Seaman pulled off a fine one-handed save from Jorg Bohme, and then Sebastian Deisler, being hailed as the bright young thing of German football, missed when left unmarked 8 yards out. That was the luck Eriksson had spoken about.

Just on half-time, however, Beckham was fouled and after his free-kick came back to him, a left-footed cross on the swivel fell for a young Steven Gerrard to drive in his first England goal. In the dressing room Eriksson told his team not to sit back, but added that as Germany pushed forward, space would open up.

So it proved, almost immediately. Beckham did well in winning the ball back and crossed, again with his left foot, allowing Emile Heskey to set up club mate Owen's second goal. His third came from another Liverpool assist, in the knowledge that Gerrard, having made an intelligent interception, would immediately lay the ball forward for him in the channel.

Well before the end, with Michael Ballack having missed badly and German supporters already heading home, Beckham sent Scholes forward into the same inside-right position and this time Heskey was the finisher, prompting the jubilant England chant 'five-one and even Heskey scored'.

It had all been enjoyed by the largest Saturday evening television audience for five years, and media reaction was naturally euphoric.

'Don't mention the score (but it's Germany 1 England 5)' was the front-page headline in the *News of the World*. The sports section had 'What a Sven-sation' with Terry Venables praising Steven Gerrard and Beckham, whose 'crosses from the right were their usual superlative selves, causing the Germans all sorts of problems'. The former England manager was one of the few to admit that 'both England and Germany were very poor in the opening half'.

One of his predecessors, Bobby Robson, called it 'the best result in England's history, no question about that,' adding 'Beckham may not be a vocal captain, but you can see the inspirational effect he has on his teammates'.

The captain told reporters,

You work for nights like this and you want to savour them. They were going to bring me off but I said I didn't want to come off. I'm absolutely loving the responsibility of being captain. The most memorable moment for me was going over to the fans at the end because the heartache that came with losing to Germany at Wembley last year was hard to come to terms with. It was a strange night for all of us. When the fourth and fifth goals went in, we all kept looking round at each other. It was funny looking at the faces. Everyone was thinking 'what the hell is going on here?'

In Monday's *Times* Oliver Holt built his piece around Beckham, revealing that there had been talk of a sweepstake in the press box about how long he would last, with 15 to 20 minutes being the most popular guess. In the event

Beckham played with a furious relish. He led his side like a wounded general ... this was unquestionably his finest hour. His continuing climb through the heights of the game defies the usual laws of football celebrity, which dictate that the more famous a player becomes, the more his hunger for excellence abates.

'Finest hour' was, of course, a big claim. A finer one would come in the white of England only a month later, but first there was a proud hour (and a half) in the red of United ...

28

Tottenham Hotspur 3 Manchester United 5
Premiership (White Hart Lane)
29 September 2001

Captain of his country for almost a year, but never of Manchester United, David Beckham was finally given that honour half a dozen games into the 2001–02 season and with a minimum of ceremony.

At dinner the night before United's game away to Tottenham, Sir Alex Ferguson simply dropped the players' complimentary match tickets into his lap for distribution – traditionally the captain's job. Ferguson told him later he had originally not been thought of as captaincy material, but had changed for the better since doing the job for England.

It was a tricky time for the manager, which would become worse during that autumn. After winning a third successive Premiership title in May, he announced his retirement for the end of the following season, by which time he would be sixty. Upset with the club's directors, he initially said it would mean cutting all ties, then two months later accepted a five-year contract to stay on as a consultant. Later he would admit to knowing almost immediately that it was wrong a) to retire and b) to announce the fact so far in advance.

A common view was that United's players took their eye off the ball in what became a trophy-less season, although Beckham felt that Steve McClaren's departure to become manager of Middlesbrough in the summer of 2001 was more significant.

Despite arriving at Tottenham in third place after half a dozen League games, there had already been problems, especially in defence. Ferguson, having spent some £47 million on Ruud van Nistelrooy and Juan Sebastian Veron, shocked everybody by selling the powerful defender Jaap Stam to Lazio, which he later admitted was also a mistake. Laurent Blanc, aged thirty-five, came in on a free transfer, but United conceded ten goals in their opening five League games, then just before the Spurs game lost to Deportivo La Coruna in the Champions League after leading with only 4 minutes to play.

Tottenham: Sullivan, Richards, King, Perry, Taricco, Freund, Anderton (Rebrov, 83), Poyet, Ziege, Ferdinand, Sheringham.

Manchester United: Barthez, G. Neville, Johnsen, Blanc, Irwin (Silvestre, 46), Beckham, Butt (Solskjaer, 40), Scholes, Veron, Cole, van Nistelrooy.
Attendance: 36,049.

If it was not to be at Old Trafford, White Hart Lane was just about the best possible venue for Beckham to wear the armband for the first time – the ground where he had first watched United all those years earlier, telling his father that he would play for them one day. Even before they knew about the captaincy, both David's parents, and Grandad Joseph, the lifelong Spurs fan, had planned to be at a game that would provide emotional turmoil for all three.

The change of captain was necessary because Roy Keane was suspended after being sent off in the previous week's dramatic 4-3 defeat at Newcastle. He was badly missed as an extraordinary first half unfolded, in which United's defence appeared to fold up.

In the 15th minute, Dean Richards marked his Tottenham debut by heading the first goal. Les Ferdinand was left completely unmarked by a misfiring offside trap to drive in the second, and just before half-time Christian Ziege was also all alone as he headed in Gus Poyet's long cross, leaving Beckham and great friend Gary Neville pointing fingers at each other. David Lacey subsequently wrote in *The Guardian*, 'it was hard to remember United giving a worse goal away during Ferguson's fiteen years'.

If the players expected their manager to be raging at half-time, they were taken by surprise. One change was made, with Denis Irwin replaced at left-back by the more adventurous Mikael Silvestre, but Andy Cole recalls him sitting there saying nothing until just before it was time to leave the dressing room, when the message was along the lines of the players knowing what they needed to do to retrieve the situation.

Ole Gunnar Solskjaer was already on as a substitute for Nicky Butt and he was widely regarded as the driving force in a second half as astonishing, and one-sided, as the first had been.

Inside less than 50 seconds, Cole had lunged forward for a diving header to score after Beckham and Neville combined down the right. Before the hour Beckham's corner was headed in by Blanc and with Spurs now defending as badly as United had done earlier, Van Nistelrooy was allowed to head the equaliser from Silvestre's cross.

The visiting support, numerous and vocal as ever in London, sensed, like the players, even greater possibilities, which materialised within a few more minutes as Veron, having one of his better games, scored with a low, left-footed drive.

There was still time for a *coup de théâtre*. Just before the end, Beckham launched an unstoppable effort past poor Neil Sullivan – the man he had beaten for his hitherto most famous goal, at Wimbledon five years earlier.
In demand from reporters in his new role as captain, he said afterwards,

Maybe we were a bit tired after Tuesday [in La Coruna], but we knew that if we could come out in the second half and get the first goal, we could go on from there. That's what the manager said and we got the goal straightaway. We've showed we are a team of character and we always recover well from setbacks.

The Sunday newspaper journalists, who would have started writing their running reports with the champions 3-0 down, were nevertheless left groping for explanations and adjectives. The *Mail on Sunday's* Joe Melling settled for

> Incredible, fantastic, the full majesty of Manchester United remains a truly magnificent sight to behold. This was reminiscent of those halcyon Busby days when Best, Charlton and Law practised their magic and results such as this and the thrilling manner in which they were achieved, were commonplace.

United's defence, he felt obliged to add, was 'a dithering mess at times'. Noting that Sven-Goran Eriksson had been among the spectators, Michael Calvin drew attention in the same paper to United's impressive England contingent and wrote, 'Whisper it around White Hart Lane but they are the type of characters who win World Cups.'

First, they had to qualify, which had come down to doing as well as Germany in the final round of group fixtures.

29

England 2 Greece 2
World Cup Qualifying Group (Old Trafford)
6 October 2001

Four days after the epic victory over Germany, England had come down to earth sufficiently to beat Albania 2-0 at Newcastle. It meant that going into the final matches, played on the same Saturday afternoon, they were level on points with the Germans and had a much better goal difference. On the assumption that Rudi Voller's team would win at home to Finland, England needed only to make sure of victory against Greece, who had just lost 5-1 in Helsinki and had nothing to play for. What could possibly go wrong?

England: Martyn, G. Neville, Ferdinand, Keown, A. Cole (McManaman, 78), Beckham, Gerrard, Scholes, Barmby (A. Cole, 46), Fowler (Sheringham, 67), Heskey.
Greece: Nikopolidis, Patsatzoglou, Dabizas, Vokolos, Costas Konstantinidis, Fissas, Zagorakis (Basinas, 57), Kassapis, Karagounis, Charisteas (Lakis, 73), Nikolaidis (Mahlas, 86).
Attendance: 66,009.

After a week of speculation, Eriksson picked Robbie Fowler rather than Andy Cole or Teddy Sheringham to replace the injured Michael Owen. With David Seaman out for several months, Nigel Martyn of Leeds was in goal and to the consternation of an expectant home crowd he soon became much the busier goalkeeper.

After one early 30-yard free-kick from Beckham brought a save from Antonis Nikopolidis, Giorgios Karagounis was close from 35 yards, Demis Nikolaidis closer still with a volley and Angelos Charisteas shot just over the bar. England could hardly complain about going in at half-time a goal behind, which arrived when right-back Christos Patsatzoglou nutmegged Ashley Cole and his cross was only cleared straight to Charisteas.

Eriksson remained as calm in the face of adversity as Ferguson had been at White Hart Lane, also making one substitution, with Andy Cole coming on at his home ground for an ineffective Barmby.

England improved, though not until Martyn had made a crucial save from the Greek captain Theo Zagorakis. Now Beckham began to exert his authority, almost recklessly, producing one of the best halves of his career.

'For some reason I had endless reserves of energy,' he said much later. 'I just got it into my head that I needed to go looking for the ball.' That involved ignoring Gary Neville, who, worried about a lack of protection down the right flank, had urged the captain to keep to the team shape.

Instead Beckham began popping up all over the pitch. Typically, he was out on the left when the Dutch referee awarded a soft free-kick for a foul on him. Teddy Sheringham, now at Tottenham, who had just replaced Fowler, knew his old club mate could pick him out from a dead ball, which was just what happened. Sheringham headed England level and with Germany still being held by Finland, England were back on track. The next shock, however, came within a few minutes. At a Greek free-kick, Rio Ferdinand hesitated and Nikolaidis scored from close in.

When the fourth official indicated 4 minutes of added time to be played, England were facing not only their first ever defeat by Greece and Eriksson's first competitive loss, but a tough play-off against Andrey Shevchenko's Ukraine rather than Belarus, as had been assumed earlier.

Small margins can decide football results. With 3 of the 4 added minutes already gone, England were awarded another soft free-kick at the Stretford End, some 28 yards out. Having hardly got a shot on target since the early one that was saved, Beckham still had the self-belief to tell Sheringham the kick was his, just as he had once done to his hero Bryan Robson of all people in an A team game for Manchester United.

He recalls hearing a single drum beating in the crowd, which provided a suitably dramatic soundtrack. Stepping slightly to the left, he hit a perfectly curving, dipping shot into the top corner of the net, the product as he rightly claimed of all those years of practice.

Perhaps those thousands of previous attempts told him too that this one was going in, which is why his ecstatic celebration seemed to begin even before the ball crossed the goalline.

What is forgotten is how quickly the euphoria around Old Trafford would have been deflated had it not been announced in the next couple of minutes that Germany too had only drawn in Gelsenkirchen, and that it was them who would have to play-off against Ukraine (who they duly beat). As it was, Beckham's has rightly gone down as one of the great individual performances, and the goal is remembered as the most famous of his seventeen for England.

Emerging from the dressing room he tried to phone Victoria, who was working in Italy, but found himself unable to speak. Meanwhile journalists were hastily rewriting the tale of an extraordinary afternoon.

The conclusion in *The Observer* was, 'This was not a great England performance but it was a performance of great character and it was fitting that David Beckham should secure the all-important point. At times the captain was almost playing Greece on his own.'

Another columnist in the same paper suggested it was a case of 'the most deserving of men capping the most tireless of performances' and the individual ratings read, 'Arguably

Coleraine 1991 (see Chapter 1): A young David Beckham exchanges pennants with the captain of Hearts before the Under-16 Milk Cup final in Northern Ireland (above); and wins his first Manchester United trophy after angering, then impressing team manager Nobby Stiles. *(Courtesy of NI Milk Cup)*

Saint-Etienne 1998 (see Chapter 18): Argentina's Diego Simeone (third left) has done his work well and Beckham's retaliation on him brings a red card and the scorn of a nation. *(Press Association)*

Barcelona 1999 (see Chapter 22): A European Cup winner after his two corners led to the most dramatic finish in the history of the competition, against a distraught Bayern Munich. *(Press Association)*

Shizuoka 2002 (see Chapter 32): Jumping out of a tackle with Roque jnr – timidly
or tactically? – that led to Brazil's equalising goal at a crucial stage of the World Cup
quarter-final *(Press Association)*

UEFA EURO 2008™ - MATCH INTERNATIONAL

STADE DE FRANCE® - SAINT-DENIS

MERCREDI 26 MARS 2008
21H00

FRANCE - ANGLETERRE

"On vit ensemble, on vibre ensemble"

ÉQUIPE DE FRANCE

Paris 2008: Beckham joins the select band of those who have won 100 caps for England. (*Author's collection*)

Manchester 2006 (see Chapter 40): Captain Beckham (front row, second left) with the England team that beat Jamaica 6-0 before setting off for an altogether tougher time at the World Cup in Germany. *(Copyright Football Association)*

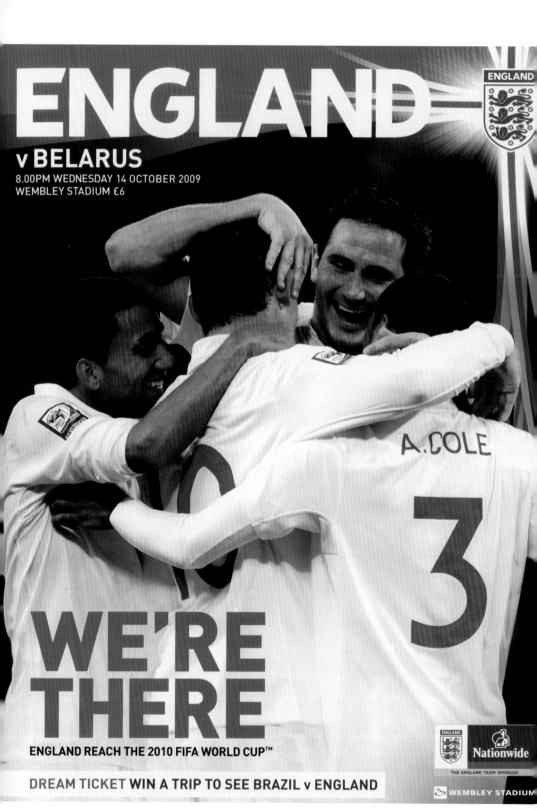

Wembley 2009 (see Chapter 45): The official programme from Beckham's 115th and final England game, against Belarus at Wembley. *(Author's collection)*

the most improved player of the lot under Eriksson, growing in stature and taking new responsibility as captain. Undeniably world-class.'

Although unable to find words for his wife, Beckham managed to tell reporters,

> It wasn't the prettiest of games but we kept fighting back. The character of the team is unbelievable. One free-kick had to go in – I was disappointed with most of them. When I got my last chance, Teddy said he would have it but I decided I'd take it.

Eriksson said of his captain:

> I knew of Beckham before I came here. But I was surprised. He is much quicker than I thought, he runs much more than I thought. He played one of the best games I have ever seen him play. He did everything today to try and push the team to win the game. Had I given up on qualifying? Of course. But if you have a corner or free-kick, with Beckham we have the best in the world.

In Monday's *Independent* Tim Rich wrote, 'There is nobody else in the world you would want to take a free-kick for your life', and amid a host of marks of four and five out of ten for other players, the paper gave him nine.

Three years on, it was further confirmation that Saint-Etienne was behind him, as the *Daily Mirror* found when sending a reporter to the South Norwood pub where his effigy had hung in the horrible aftermath of that night. Bar manager Anne Marie Callear was quoted as saying, 'If he had come in here a few years ago he would have been lynched. If he paid a visit now he wouldn't be allowed to buy a drink all night and everyone would treat him like a hero.'29 to

30

Manchester United 3 Deportivo La Coruna 2
Champions League Quarter-Final Second Leg
(Old Trafford)
10 April 2002

However hard international footballers try to concentrate on their club during a World Cup year, the summer festival is rarely far from their thoughts. So each time David Beckham was badly hurt in the two legs of the Champions League quarter-final, the possibility of missing out on England's trip to Japan and South Korea loomed large in his mind.

Manchester United and Deportivo La Coruna, having never met before, saw an awful lot of each other during the 2001–02 season. Initially drawn together in the qualifying group, they played two eventful games both won by the Spaniards – 2-1 at home with a pair of late goals and, even more shockingly, 3-2 at Old Trafford a month later with a blunder by goalkeeper Fabien Barthez.

Sir Alex Ferguson was implementing a new style of play for Europe, with Ruud van Nistelrooy effectively a lone striker, normally backed up by Paul Scholes just behind him, while Roy Keane sat deep in front of the back four. By the second group stage it appeared to be working more effectively, bringing two draws against Bayern Munich and qualification for a quarter-final against Deportivo. This time defensive discipline was much better in the away game, a 2-0 win with goals by Van Nistelrooy and Beckham, a 30-yarder that was 'one of my all-time favourite United goals' and his sixteenth of the season.

More worrying was the injury he sustained just before the end when caught heavily on the ankle by Diego Tristan and forced to leave the ground on crutches. A scan found nothing worse than bad bruising, but the relief would prove short-lived.

Manchester United: Barthez, G. Neville, Blanc, Johnsen (Brown, 36), Silvestre, Beckham (Solskjaer, 22), Veron (P. Neville, 73), Butt, Fortune, Van Nistelrooy Giggs.
Deportivo: Molina, Scaloni, Romero, Duscher, Naybet, Hector, Victor (Makaay, 50), Valeron, Diego Tristan, (Pandani, 72), Fran (Capdevila, 62), Djalminha.
Attendance: 65,875.

On a night when United's advancement to the Champions League semi-final was never in serious doubt, the most dramatic moment concerned none of the five goals but a tussle for the ball midway through the first half. David Beckham has estimated that the chances of winning it were sixty/forty in his favour and is insistent that the Argentine midfielder Pedro Duscher arrived late, two-footed and with his studs up, catching him on the left foot just after Beckham had nicked the ball away.

Initially hoping against hope that he might be able to play on, he reluctantly came to the conclusion quicker than the United doctor bending over him: 'It's broken'. United supporters, traditionally not great England fans, might have been immediately more concerned about the effect on their club's quest for the European Cup and diminishing hopes of beating Arsenal to the Premiership title. They had little to worry about from Deportivo, Ole Gunnar Solskjaer arriving as Beckham's replacement on the night to score two goals and ease the passage into the last four.

Veron created both of them, on either side of Laurent Blanc's own goal, Ryan Giggs made it 3-1 and although Djalminha scored right at the end, Duscher (after two further fouls on Van Nistelrooy and Butt) and Lionel Scaloni had by then both been sent off.

But the story of the night was on the front pages of the next day's newspapers, *The Independent* headlining 'World Cup fears after Beckham breaks foot' and adding that he was 'likely to miss the World Cup finals ... a devastating blow to England, who only reached the tournament after a series of inspirational performances by Beckham'.

Even the paper's chief sportswriter, James Lawton, who a year later would describe Beckham as 'the most overrated footballer in the history of the game', admitted the injury had 'the damage potential of a cluster bomb' to England's hopes.

With the opening game against Sweden just under two months away, Ferguson tantalisingly estimated he would be out for between six and eight weeks. Asked how much of a blow this was to England, the manager responded tartly: 'It's a blow to Manchester United'.

In that, Ferguson (who had announced in February that he would not be retiring after all, despite Sven-Goran Eriksson having been offered his job), was quite right. Beckham was not able to play again that season for his club, who unexpectedly lost the Champions League semi-final on away goals to Bayer Leverkusen and then conceded the Premiership to Arsenal, finishing behind Liverpool too in third place.

Meanwhile, the nation became familiar with the word 'metatarsal' – all the more so when Gary Neville suffered exactly the same injury against Leverkusen. That left him with no chance of making the World Cup, while the verdict on Beckham continued to be debated.

Lightweight modern boots were widely blamed for the injury and the day after the Deportivo game, Christopher Bulstrode, Professor of Orthopaedics at Oxford University, was quoted as saying 'this could end his career'. Others were less dramatic, including the doctor who took Beckham's x-rays at the Manchester Royal Infirmary and told him he should make the World Cup – just.

The feverish mood in the country at large was summed up in two incidents. *The Sun,* which had reacted with contempt to Glenn Hoddle's use of the faith healer Eileen Drewery, printed a full-page picture of Beckham's foot and asked readers to place their hands on it. And the Prime Minister, Tony Blair, was said by his official spokesman to have raised the matter at a Cabinet meeting otherwise dominated by the Middle East. (It was not immediately clear which issue had caused the greater concern).

31

England 1 Argentina 0
World Cup (Sapporo)
7 June 2002

If fortune favoured the brave in the last tumultuous minute of England's World Cup qualifying campaign, their luck seemed to be running out thereafter.

When the draw was made in December, Sven-Goran Eriksson confided that the three teams he wanted to avoid were Argentina, France and Italy. England were duly thrown together with what he called the best team in South America, as well as Nigeria ('maybe the best in Africa') and his own country, Sweden, who England had only drawn with at Old Trafford the previous month thanks to a David Beckham penalty.

Furthermore, by the time Eriksson named his squad of twenty-three early in May, Beckham and Gary Neville had both broken their foot, and on the last day of the Premiership season, Steven Gerrard, just emerging as a serious talent at international level, was ruled out, to be followed later in the month by the first proposed replacement, Danny Murphy – a third metatarsal victim.

The weekend before the opening group match against Sweden, one Sunday newspaper headlined 'Bye-bye Beckham', but in fact his fitness was slowly improving, along with that of Kieron Dyer – another player whose participation in the tournament had been in considerable doubt.

In the end Beckham played for the first 62 minutes and Dyer replaced him in a 1-1 draw; the captain took the corner that was headed in by Sol Campbell to put England ahead, but in the second half they fell back too far, leaving Michael Owen isolated and hitting long balls upfield that brought some furious criticism from the press. Eriksson had to tell his downcast players afterwards 'It's not a funeral' and start lifting them for the key game at the indoor stadium of Sapporo.

He chose a team that looked better balanced, with Heskey moved from the problem position on the left of midfield to replace Darius Vassell in attack, making room for Nicky Butt alongside Owen Hargreaves in central midfield.

England: Seaman, Mills, Campbell, Ferdinand, A. Cole, Beckham, Hargreaves (Sinclair, 19), Butt, Scholes, Owen (Bridge, 80), Heskey (Sheringham, 55).

Argentina: Cavallero, Pochettino, Samuel, Placente, Zanetti, Simeone, Veron (Aimar, 46), Sorin, Ortega, Batistuta (Crespo, 60), Gonzalez (Lopez, 65).
Attendance: 35,927.

In a phone call before the match, Victoria Beckham told her husband, 'don't do anything stupid, will you?' About half of each team remained from 1998 in Saint-Etienne, including Juan Sebastian Veron, who was now a Manchester United teammate, and Beckham's nemesis Diego Simeone. An obvious subject for the pre-match interviews, England's captain Beckham was not afraid to revisit the occasion, telling the press, 'That haunted me for a while. It was the biggest downer of my career. But when pressure is thrown at me, I can kick it straight back.'

He could not, however, have imagined how much pressure would be placed on him a minute before half-time.

England's satisfaction at seeing the Italian Pierluigi Collina appointed as referee was underlined when he showed a yellow card to Gabriel Batistuta for clattering into Ashley Cole after only 12 minutes. An even earlier collision, when Michael Owen ran into Owen Hargreaves, was potentially disruptive and soon forced Hargreaves off, but the change proved a positive one: the more attacking Trevor Sinclair came on, allowing Scholes to move inside, forming a familiar Manchester United triangle with Beckham and the deeper-lying Butt.
They performed so well together that Veron, Argentina's captain, was taken off at half-time after making no headway against them.

Midway through the first half Butt's long pass sent Owen darting through to hit the inside of the far post and on another jinking run just before the interval he was tripped by the long-haired Mauricio Pochettino – later to be the manager of Southampton and Tottenham – and went down to earn a penalty.

Owen asked Beckham, who he said looked nervous, if he was happy to take it. Nervous or not, the captain had demons to put to flight once and for all, and placed the ball. Simeone tried to distract him with an outstretched hand but was dragged away by minders Butt and Scholes.

If Bayern in the Champions League final was his most important corner- kick (twice) and Greece his most vital free-kick, this was surely the most crucial penalty of Beckham's career. Imagine the headlines if he insisted on taking it instead of Owen but missed and England lost: 'One Stupid Boy' again?

The photo of the kick is worth including in any book of skills: eyes on the ball, left foot alongside it, arms out for balance, leaning sufficiently far back to drive the shot hard as was his aim but not to sky it. Owen and two Argentine defenders were preparing to rush forward for any rebound, but there would not be one. Having put his last two penalties for United straight down the middle, Beckham did not worry about whether the Argentine goalkeeper Pablo Cavallero had done his homework, sending this one in the same place, but with enough of a thump to defeat him.

The wildness of his celebration, racing towards the corner-flag and kissing the Three Lions badge, was reminiscent of Stuart Pearce's relief and redemption after scoring in the shoot-out against Spain at Euro 96.

It was probably just as well that the half-time whistle blew soon afterwards to enable everyone to calm down just a little. England had played some excellent football and it continued in the second half, with Owen's runs still troubling the South Americans, four years after he made his name against them.

Moving past Placente, he hit a shot just wide of the far post, before Scholes had a superb 25-yard volley punched out by the goalkeeper, who then had to save a volley from substitute Teddy Sheringham.

There was only one nasty moment for England, when Pochettino almost redeemed himself with a header from a corner, blocked right on the line by David Seaman and hacked away by Sheringham.

Eriksson sent on Wayne Bridge for Owen to help shore things up, leaving Sheringham as the only striker, but there were no further alarms before England's thousands of supporters – backed up by many more Japanese – could celebrate a victory that kept them level with Sweden in the Group F table.

With reporters swarming round him, Beckham said of his penalty,

I must admit it was an emotional time when the ball went in. It was the sweetest moment of my career. After what happened last time the game meant so much to me and my family. To the whole country in fact. As a footballing nation we'd been waiting for that result for a long time. Germany was a massive result for us but there is a lot of history to England v Argentina.

32

Brazil 2 England 1
World Cup Quarter-Final (Shizuoka)
21 June 2002

Well deserved and rapturously celebrated as it was, England's win over Argentina took a lot out of them. Five days later, in temperatures of 93 degrees, they managed only a goalless draw against Nigeria in the final group game, when a win, it transpired, would have opened up an easier path through the knockout stages.

Denmark held few fears for Eriksson's team in the second round and were duly dismissed 3-0, all the goals coming in a one-sided first half. Two days after that, however, it was confirmed that the quarter-final opponents would be Brazil, winners for the fourth time in 1994 and beaten finalists in 1998.

Watching them win 2-0 against Belgium, who had a goal wrongly disallowed at 0-0, England's players and staff – not to mention the media – were encouraged by how vulnerable the Brazilian defence looked, with Roque Jnr in the centre identified as a weak link. Even the great Pele, while never as good a pundit as he was a footballer, suggested that England had the best defence in the competition and that he was worried by David Beckham and Michael Owen.

What he did not know was that neither of those two key players was anything like fully fit. Against Denmark Owen had come off at half-time with a combination of groin and hamstring strain and Beckham had taken another painful knock to his left foot.

Eriksson, while encouraged by how well Belgium had stood up to the Brazilians, was fully aware of the danger threatened by a combination of Rivaldo and Ronaldo, who had scored the goals against them, plus of course the younger Ronaldinho. His instructions to an unchanged England were to be compact and work as a unit 'otherwise they will kill us'.

Luiz Felipe Scolari, meanwhile, stuck with his attacking wing-backs Cafu and Roberto Carlos, but brought in an extra defensive midfielder in Kleberson to protect the suspect central defensive trio.

Older fans were perhaps reminded of when the teams met at the 1970 World Cup, with Pele and Jairzinho confronted by Bobby Moore and Gordon Banks. Now, once again, it was the tournament's best attack against its best defence.

Brazil: Marcos, Cafu, Lucio, Edmilson, Roque Jnr, Kleberson, Roberto Carlos, Gilberto Silva, Ronaldinho, Ronaldo (Edison, 70), Rivaldo.
England: Seaman, Mills, Ferdinand, Campbell, Cole (Sheringham, 80), Beckham, Butt, Scholes, Sinclair (Dyer, 56), Owen (Vassell, 79), Heskey.
Attendance: 47,436.

The first disappointment for Eriksson's men was that the previous day's torrential rain had been replaced by 86-degree heat, the effect of which could only be imagined by England supporters back at home waking up for the 7.30 a.m. kick-off. After an opening 20 minutes quiet enough to put many of them back to sleep, the country's biggest match for sixteen years came alive with a save by David Seaman from Ronaldo and then a goal for England.

Owen, unable even to walk at one point on the day before the game, had decided he would simply hang around the penalty area hoping to pick up pieces, which was precisely what happened in the 24th minute. Lucio justified doubts about Brazil's defence by allowing Emile Heskey's long ball to bounce off his thigh into the path of Owen, who was suddenly not feeling his injury as he ran on to beat Marcos.

There is a widely held belief that if England had maintained their lead until half-time, they would have won the game, and gone on to defeat Turkey in the semi-final and one of the weaker German teams of recent times in the final to become World Cup winners. Such a conviction is dependent on an awful lot of assumptions, but whether sustainable or not, it became irrelevant because of one of the most controversial moments of David Beckham's career – one that his sternest critics have held against him ever since.

In the last minute of the half, he challenged Kleberson near the touchline and as the ball ran loose Roque Jnr and Roberto Carlos closed in on it, whereupon Beckham jumped out of the way. Was he concerned, even subconsciously, about his foot? His argument has always been that he was convinced the ball was going out of play and that by the time England slowly took the throw-in, the Mexican referee would end the first half.

Now Brazil had possession. Paul Scholes might have won it back, but failed to stop Ronaldinho, who then went past Ashley Cole with a step-over and fed Rivaldo in Cole's left-back position for an immaculately placed first-time drive curled low beyond Seaman.

Only in retrospect was the move traced back to Beckham, and as Danny Mills, England's right-back who would have taken the throw-in, points out, a lot happened between that moment and the goal:

I don't think he jumped out of a tackle, he jumped to let the ball go out of play. But that was about 70 yards from goal. Ronaldinho goes on and on and then it falls to Rivaldo, with possibly the best left foot on the planet at that time, who rolls it into the corner.

What most England players agree on is that they could have done with a rousing half-time speech. But neither the manager nor the captain, were noted for those. As one of the squad – the erudite Gareth Southgate has always denied it was him – put it, 'We needed Winston Churchill and we got [Tory party leader] Iain Duncan Smith.' Mills added,

If we'd gone in 1-0 up, you can breathe, reorganise, you've got something to hang onto. But you go in at half-time demoralised, and then we didn't get the kick up the backside, that motivational speech, that we needed. We just didn't have that big speech like a Mourinho or a Ferguson would have done.

The force was with Brazil and only 5 minutes into the second half Ronaldinho's long free-kick from way out on the right completely deceived David Seaman and landed in the net. Whether he meant it, as he initially claimed, has never been clearly established.

If England felt even wearier at that point there was unexpected new hope soon afterwards in the shape of a red card for Ronaldinho for catching Mills, who cheerfully admits to staying down and making the most of the foul.

The next 30 minutes could have been among the most famous in English football history, but brought only frustration and a lesson from ten opponents in how to keep the ball. By the time of the final whistle England had managed one shot on target other than Owen's goal in the whole match.

It was a bitter disappointment, well summed up by *The Daily Telegraph's* Henry Winter:

> Sven-Goran Eriksson insisted there were 'no regrets' but the haunted look worn by each of his players told another story. They knew they had wasted a golden chance of reaching the World Cup semi-finals, had committed errors allowing Brazil to snatch the lead and then failed to pursue depleted opponents intelligently. No regrets? Regrets stained the players' faces like teardrops.

In *The Sun*, Alan Shearer made the valid point that England didn't force enough scoring chances in the whole competition. Terry Venables' lament was also destined to become a familiar one down the years: 'The key was to keep the ball when we were 1-0 up but we just kept knocking it up and giving it back to them.'

Eriksson would not admit it at the time but years later his autobiography questioned whether the players ever really believed they could win the game. Sol Campbell, a star in defence with Rio Ferdinand, has admitted the same thing.

As for Beckham, it was universally acknowledged that he had not been properly fit at any stage. As Eriksson's trusty assistant Tord Grip said, 'We hoped David would get better as the tournament went on but it never happened. He was always the same – about 75 per cent of his normal game.'

33

Manchester United 0 Arsenal 2
FA Cup Fifth Round (Old Trafford)
15 February 2003

As previous chapters have suggested, there are different points at which Sir Alex Ferguson's relationship with David Beckham started breaking down. There can be little doubt about the occasion on which it collapsed completely.

Further warning signs had been apparent all season, the first three months of which Beckham has described as his worst at the club. After a month of barely speaking to him, Ferguson made the most hurtful of accusations in questioning his loyalty to Manchester United, for having gone to meet the Queen at Buckingham Palace with the England squad rather than going on holiday to rest a broken rib. Later, even Sandra Beckham confronted the manager, to her son's embarrassment.

There were personal problems too, including the deeply upsetting news that his parents were divorcing and then a kidnap threat to Victoria and the two children (baby Romeo had been born in September).

For the first time in his career Beckham was not happy either training or playing, the irony being that United looked as if this could turn into a season to match or even eclipse the Treble year. After a sluggish start they were second in the table behind Arsenal, through to the Worthington Cup final against Liverpool, and progressing comfortably in the Champions League, the final of which was to be played at Old Trafford.

In the FA Cup, Portsmouth and West Ham had been dismissed imperiously by 4-1 and 6-0 to bring Arsenal themselves to Manchester. The fifth round tie was the most obvious of choices for BBC's live Saturday lunchtime television coverage and yet the cameras would miss the greatest drama of all.

Manchester United: Barthez, G Neville, Brown, Ferdinand, Silvestre, Beckham (Butt, 83), Keane, Scholes, Solskjaer, Van Nistelrooy, Giggs (Forlan, 71)
Arsenal: Seaman, Lauren, Keown, Campbell, Cole, Parlour, Edu, Vieira, Pires (Van Bronckhorst, 83), Jeffers (Henry, 73), Wiltord (Toure, 90).
Attendance: 67,209.

Although both clubs had a Champions League game to play the following midweek, it was Arsenal who chose to field a weakened team, surprisingly leaving Dennis Berkamp out altogether and Thierry Henry among their substitutes. The perception was that Bergkamp would be unsuited to the highly physical nature of games between the country's two leading teams, which is exactly how things turned out. As the *Manchester Evening News* recorded, 'what had been billed as a potential classic quickly erupted into an ugly, spiteful contest where skill and precision took a back seat to aggression and force'.

Referee Jeff Winter tried to clamp down from the start by booking Paul Scholes, Ruud van Nistelrooy and Arsenal's Patrick Vieira all within the first 7 minutes. In a throwback to the old days, he then felt obliged to call together the two captains, Roy Keane and Vieira, and tell them to get a grip of their teams. Keane still picked up the next yellow card himself, for fouling Robert Pires.

When some football broke out, the key moment was an extraordinary miss by Ryan Giggs. A superb long pass by Beckham left Martin Keown and his goalkeeper David Seaman stranded, but Giggs, after rounding the goalkeeper, shot over an open goal from the edge of the penalty area. Worse for United, after 32 minutes Wes Brown fouled Vieira and Edu's free-kick deflected off United's defensive wall into the net.

The incident that would lead, four months later, to David Beckham leaving Manchester United occurred in the 52nd minute. Edu ran with the ball from midfield and fed Sylvain Wiltord; the Frenchman, whose goal had sealed the Double at Old Trafford for Arsenal the previous season, cut inside and again finished well. As United struggled vainly to get back into the contest, Beckham limped off after being caught with a heavy tackle by England teammate Ashley Cole.

What happened when the home team's players reached the dressing room did not emerge until two days later. In the meantime the reaction was standard knockabout fare: Arsene Wenger claimed of United, 'They tried to intimidate us but we kept our heads'; Ferguson blamed Jeff Winter, saying 'You need the referee to be able to handle it and he reacted badly. He allowed the Arsenal players to bully him.'

The only news lines appeared to be that any chance of an unprecedented quadruple triumph were now over and that Beckham was considered doubtful for the following Wednesday's Champions League game at home to Juventus. That was until the appearance of Monday morning's *Sun,* whose huge front-page headline, one word under the other, read, 'Fergie decks Becks'.

It was only a slight exaggeration, like the sports section headlining 'Fergie nearly left him blind', and reporting 'there are fears the England captain could walk out of the club'. What most eyewitness accounts, including those of the two protagonists, have subsequently come to agree upon is roughly as follows:

Ferguson, never the best of losers, especially to Wenger's Arsenal, arrived in the dressing room and immediately criticised Beckham, as he had already done at half-time. Now the accusation was that he had not chased Edu sufficiently before the second goal. The film of the match tends to bear out this view, although as with Brazil's winning goal at the

World Cup, there were a number of teammates around who could also have intervened – a point Beckham quickly made in response.

Fed up with what he now regarded as Ferguson's constant carping, he found all the frustrations of the previous months coming to the fore and committed the sin of swearing at his boss. It was at that point that Ferguson, once a mean centre-forward, swung a foot at a boot lying on the floor which struck him just above the left eye from around 12 feet away.

Feeling blood, an astonished and infuriated Beckham moved bravely towards his manager, only to be held back, wisely, by a couple of players. He spat out some blood, not as was reported at Ferguson, but on the floor, then went next door to have the cut stitched. Either before or after that, the manager clearly said 'I'm sorry', but the damage had been done – in every sense.

From then on, everything became a public relations exercise, in which Beckham made sure he was photographed in an Alice band, sticking plaster clearly visible across his stitches, but also put out a statement ahead of the Juventus game emphasising 'it's all in the past'. It was not, of course, for as Ferguson himself has said, it was after that incident that he told Manchester United's board Beckham had to go.

34

Manchester United 4 Real Madrid 3
(Madrid won 6-5 on Aggregate)
Champions League Quarter-Final Second Leg
(Old Trafford)
23 April 2003

Tempting as it might have been to leave Beckham out of the Juventus match immediately after what inevitably came to be dubbed 'Bootgate', Ferguson resisted, and was rewarded when he rose to the occasion by making both goals for Wes Brown and Ruud van Nistelrooy as the crowd pointedly chanted his name in a 2-1 win. 'David Beckham let his own boots do the talking last night,' reported the *Manchester Evening News*.

An outstanding 3-0 victory in Turin the following week assured United of a place in the quarter-final, where their opponents would be old adversaries Real Madrid, who had finished only second in their group to AC Milan but looked formidable opponents.

They proved it early in April, winning their home leg 3-1 in front of a 75,000 crowd with a superb display of what *The Times* called 'fantasy football'. United's only consolation was a Van Nistelrooy goal after they had gone 3-0 down in under 50 minutes to a side who left out Steve McManaman while including such *galacticos* as Zinedine Zidane, Luis Figo and Ronaldo.

Now the talk was that come the end of the season, David Beckham would join them. Indeed, several Real players had told the club's president Florentino Perez to sign him. He did not enhance his prospects with his performance in Madrid, easily subdued by Roberto Carlos after suffering a tight hamstring early on. On the following Saturday he was unfit for United's game at Newcastle, which they won 6-2 to go top of the table with a stunning performance, enabling Beckham's critics to point out that for many of their better efforts that season he was either a substitute or not involved at all.

Ole Gunnar Solskjaer had come in at St James' Park, and for Ferguson it was an easy decision to keep him there at Beckham's expense for the crucial 2-2 draw away to title rivals Arsenal four days later. On the Saturday Beckham was back for a home win against Blackburn, only to be dropped again for the game that mattered more, against Madrid. Dismayed, for the first time he seriously contemplated what it would be like playing for another club.

Manchester United: Barthez, O'Shea, Ferdinand, Brown, Silvestre (Phil Neville, 79), Solskjaer, Veron (Beckham, 63), Butt, Keane (Fortune, 82), Van Nistelrooy, Giggs.

Real Madrid: Casillas, Salgado, Hierro, Helguera, Carlos, Zidane, McManaman (Portillo, 69), Figo (Pavon, 88), Makelele, Ronaldo (Solari, 67), Guti.
Attendance: 66,708.

Paul Scholes, like Gary Neville, was unavailable after collecting another yellow card in the away leg, and what particularly irked Beckham was not that the ever-reliable and in-form Solskjaer should start but that Juan Sebastian Veron should come into the centre of midfield after missing the previous seven weeks through injury.

It was Veron that Beckham replaced just after the hour mark, by which point Madrid led 3-2 on the night and therefore 6-3 on aggregate. He had every incentive to make a point and did so.

United's prospects of reaching the semi-final dimmed after only 12 minutes when Ronaldo, who would become the star of the night, beat Barthez at his near post. The passionate home crowd dared to hope again when Van Nistelrooy, on an apparently unstoppable scoring run in all competitions, equalised just before half-time from Solskjaer's pass.

The key was to stop Madrid scoring again, since two away goals would mean United had to score five for victory. Their defence remained shaky, however, and early in the second half Zidane started a move that led to Ronaldo converting Roberto Carlos' cross.

Salvaging something on the night was now the best United could hope for. Helguero inadvertently helped them by turning Veron's harmless shot into his own net, but before the hour Ronaldo completed his hat-trick.

Exit the Brazilian, to a standing ovation; enter Beckham, equalising with what he regarded as his best-ever free-kick for United and then touching in a winning goal in the 84th minute. After swapping shirts with Zidane, he took a bare-chested bow to all four corners of the ground, wondering how many more European nights he would have on his favourite pitch.

Press reports struck a generally unified note, typified by Matt Lawton's verdict on United in the *Daily Mail*:

> ... a valiant effort, one that restored pride in the face of yet more European failure, but against an outstanding Real Madrid they were too often outclassed. Ferguson was left to reflect on a selection gamble that failed to pay off. Beckham's omission remained a strange one, especially when Juan Sebastian Veron returned from a seven-week absence with a knee injury.

In the next day's *Mail* he was back in the news pages for going shopping, which was somehow considered to be a public show of defiance. The sports pages reported that Barthez, blamed for the first goal, would leave at the end of the season and that Beckham's 'interest in a move to Real this summer has grown considerably in the last week or so'. A two-page spread headlined 'Wily Fergie can't let him leave' listed five reasons to go and five to stay, including 'he loves United'.

In the same paper Jeff Powell claimed Ferguson was deliberately provoking Beckham because he now needed goading to produce his best performances: The United manager won the match by getting the best out of Beckham in one short, intense, concentrated spasm of incensed ego.

Madrid's manager, Vicente del Bosque, however, had been delighted Beckham was left out until the last half-an-hour – a decision he found 'extraordinary'. He later told journalist John Carlin for a fascinating book about Beckham and Real Madrid:

God knows what might have happened if he had played from the start. He was so inspired, so wired up. Extraordinary that Ferguson left him on the bench or did not bring him on earlier. Had a Spanish coach done that in a game of that magnitude, he'd have been fired. No doubt about it.

Inevitable controversy or not, all agreed it had been a wonderful night's football. Referee Pierluigi Collina called it the best game he had ever seen. Equally impressed was a little-known Russian oligarch called Roman Abramovich, who decided that night that he wanted some of this excitement and must buy a club. Within a couple of months he did so, choosing Chelsea and changing the face of English football.

What was galling for United was to watch Juventus – a team they had beaten twice in the group stage – knock out Real Madrid in the semi-final and go on to defeat AC Milan in the final on what should have been United's own Old Trafford stage.

35

Everton 1 Manchester United 3
Premiership (Goodison Park)
11 May 2003

Out of the Champions League and beaten by Liverpool in the Worthington Cup final, United again had 'only' the championship of England to play for. Desperate to avoid a second successive trophy-less season, Sir Alex Ferguson could have done without the constant speculation about David Beckham's future, which on one occasion prompted an obscenity laden rant at a radio reporter who dared ask the question everyone wanted answering.

The fact was that the manager had already made up his mind that Beckham should be transferred. Only four days after the Real Madrid game, the *Sunday Times* ran a feature in its news section headed 'El Becks. What awaits England's captain in Madrid?' which proved premature but prophetic.

The player's own emotions were all over the place. On a high after his late intervention against Madrid and unable to sleep, he sat and watched a rerun of the whole game, only to become upset by the sight of Ferguson's 'rage' when he put one free-kick over the bar.

After the final home game, in which United beat Charlton 4-1, Beckham took little Brooklyn onto the pitch for a kick about, believing it might well have been his last match there. But his feelings would change again a week later, when they went to Goodison Park as champions for the sixth time in eight seasons.

Everton: Wright, Hibbert, Yobo, Stubbs, Unsworth, Watson, Carsley, Gravesen (Chadwick, 72), Naysmith (Pistone, 80), Campbell (Ferguson, 40), Rooney.
Manchester United: Carroll, Brown (P. Neville, 40), Ferdinand, Silvestre, O'Shea (Blanc, 46), Beckham, Keane, Scholes, Giggs, Solskjaer (Fortune, 75), Van Nistelrooy.
Attendance: 40,168

Although Arsenal had conceded the title with an unexpected home defeat by Leeds the day after United beat Charlton, it was a big game for David Moyes' Everton, striving to qualify for European football for the first time since 1996. They lay sixth, needing to hold off Blackburn, who were 2 points behind them and away to Spurs.

An early goal offered them every hope, when Kevin Campbell lost Mikael Silvestre and Solskjaer to head them in front. Where Ferguson and Beckham were united, however, was in wanting to avoid an anticlimax on this particular day, and just before half-time with United right back in the game, David hit a curling, diagonal free-kick past Richard Wright.

In the second half a teenage striker called Wayne Rooney began to trouble the champions without managing to take any of his chances and after Wright kept out one further Beckham effort, Ruud van Nistelrooy hit the bar and then picked himself up to score from the penalty spot following a foul on him by Alan Stubbs. It was the tenth successive Premiership game in which he had scored, and his twenty-fifth goal of the season, enabling him to pip Arsenal's Thierry Henry by one for the Golden Boot.

When Mike Riley blew the final whistle, Beckham was able to celebrate with his pals, suddenly feeling part of it all again and not wanting to play anywhere else. Up in the stand, however, his father sensed that he was watching his son in a United shirt for the last time.

The newspapers tended to concentrate on Everton's disappointment at missing out on Europe, Blackburn having won 4-0 at Tottenham to climb above them. But in *The Independent* Phil Shaw praised Beckham's 'superlative equaliser' and wrote,

> Like true champions Manchester United kept going right to the end, coming from behind to outclass Everton and deny David Moyes' side a UEFA Cup place. If the decisive penalty award was questionable, there was no doubting United's superiority.

Twenty years to the day after leading Aberdeen to victory in the European Cup-Winners Cup final against Real Madrid, Ferguson had yet another trophy to savour. 'It's been a great season for the club – we showed hunger right until the end,' he said. Moyes conceded, 'We've been beaten by a brilliant free-kick and a soft penalty, but you end up where you deserve to be'.

The question that the scorer of that free-kick was asking himself as he flew off to South Africa with England was where he was going to end up, or deserved to be.

To his surprise, United suddenly offered a new, improved contract, but without giving him the impression they were sincere in wanting him to stay. Although aware that United and his agent Tony Stephens were talking to clubs in Italy and Spain, he was then stunned and justifiably angry on 10 June when United put out a statement saying they had received an acceptable offer from Barcelona.

Beckham's own statement said in reply that he felt he was being used 'as a political pawn in the Barcelona presidential elections', but he could now see the writing on the Old Trafford walls. Real Madrid had in fact been given permission to talk to Stephens almost a month earlier, and the knowledge that arch-rivals Barcelona were in the hunt spurred them on. Fortunately, Beckham had decided after long discussions with his family that Madrid would be the destination of choice.

On 15 June (two days after being awarded an OBE), he spoke to Real's president Florentino Perez by telephone, and two days later the deal that had once been denied by both clubs was done. While United thought they were playing hardball in holding out for £25million, the Spanish club's director of marketing, Jose Angel Sanchez, regarded the fee as *'cacahuetes'* – peanuts – admitting later that he would have paid far more. Real Madrid and their major sponsors knew the value of David Beckham, on the field and (crucially) off it.

36

Real Madrid 2 Betis 1
La Liga (Santiago Bernabeu)
30 August 2003

Even before David Beckham kicked a football as a Real Madrid player, the club were rubbing their hands. The day after his official signing they sold 8,000 replica shirts adorned with the number 23 (chosen in homage to basketball superstar Michael Jordan). That was four times as many as Ronaldo had shifted and twenty-five times as many as Zinedine Zidane. On an exhausting pre-season tour to China, Japan and Thailand he was mobbed everywhere, justifying all the commercial department's hopes of exploiting the Asian market.

Once the football started, his high-profile teammates, not easily impressed, quickly appreciated his work ethic, ability on the ball and tactical intelligence. A typical goal direct from a free-kick against FC Tokyo confirmed he would be the set-piece expert. Just as important, as one of them put it, he was 'a good guy'.

Whatever the dressing room thought, a couple of far less impressive Beckham performances in a friendly at Valencia (0-0) and the first leg of the Spanish Super Cup away to Mallorca (lost 2-1) saw him substituted twice and under pressure ahead of his home debut in the second leg. But long before the end he had the crowd chanting his name, had scored his first goal (with a header of all things) and collected his first medal following a 3-0 win.

'Brilliant Becks fully deserves his head-lines' said the *Daily Express*. The front page of *Marca,* Madrid's sports paper sometimes described as Real's house-magazine, went with 'Beckham conquers the Bernabeu'. But now for La Liga.

Real Madrid: Casillas, Salgado, Helguera, Raul Bravo, Roberto Carlos, Beckham, Cambiasso, Zidane (Portillo, 75), Figo, Raul (Solari, 73), Ronaldo (Morientes, 85).
Real Betis: Contreras, Varela (Ito, 85), Lembo, Juanito, Mingo, Arzu, Lopez, Joaquin, Assuncao, (Fernando, 60) , Capi, Palermo (Maldonado, 70).
Attendance: 60,000.

Not untypically, Madrid had fired their manager Vicente del Bosque, despite winning the Spanish League and reaching the Champions League semi-final with those dazzling performances against Manchester United. In his place came Carlos Queiroz, who had been Sir Alex Ferguson's assistant that year, and was prepared to move as big a star as Luis Figo in order to accommodate Beckham in his United position on the right of midfield. Figo shifted to the left, with Zinedine Zidane inside him, Raul and Ronaldo up front and Esteban Cambiasso (who a dozen years later would be doing the same job for Leicester City) as the one defensive midfielder.

In retrospect, the opening La Liga game could be seen as the story of Beckham's first season in Spain, if not all four of them: some dazzling attacking play by the team's *galacticos* undermined by defensive weakness in midfield and at the back.

Amid all the excitement of the Englishman's arrival, inadequate attention was paid to a departure in the opposite direction: not Steve McManaman, leaving after four years for Manchester City, but Claude Makelele, joining Chelsea because under the new Abramovich regime they were able to pay him more money than even Real Madrid. It took barely one match to show how much he would be missed.

Beckham's start was dreamlike, not least for featuring so many of Madrid's superstars. Zidane turns and feeds Ronaldo. Figo's run takes defenders away as the Brazilian plays a one-two with Raul and his low cross is perfect for the onrushing Beckham to side-foot into the net from 4 yards out.

Immediately he rushes over and leaps into Ronaldo's arms (providing the front-cover photograph for John Carlin's book). Barely a couple of minutes into his La Liga career, he is already on the scoresheet and in two home games has scored with those least familiar Beckham goals – a header and a tap-in.

It was not long before worrying signs appeared, when Betis' new striker from Villarreal, the Argentine Martin Palermo, was left unmarked to head against the bar. Only a few minutes later, unmarked once more, he headed the equaliser from Juanito's corner.

No matter. Clean sheets are considered less important to this team than simply outscoring the opposition. How can they fail to, with this line-up? At the start of the second half Beckham, watched by his wife and father, smashes a 30-yard drive against the bar, bringing one of those long drawn-out Spanish 'ooooooh's from the crowd. Soon one of his classic long diagonal passes from right to left finds Zidane, whose cross is run in by Ronaldo. It proves the winning goal, although only thanks to some fine saves by Iker Casillas in goal.

The visiting English media contingent were impressed – perhaps even a little proud – although the more perceptive tempered their praise with caution about Madrid's defensive weakness. The *Independent on Sunday* observed, 'If the story began as a fairy-tale, with a goal after just 126 seconds, before turning into a bit of a horror yarn as Madrid were alarmingly overrun by Real Betis in a cameo of their shortcomings, it had the right ending.'

In the *Daily Express*, Graham Hunter wrote,

The England captain imposed himself against a stubborn, talented and occasionally thuggish Real Betis side and eventually emerged as the most significant player on the pitch. After the fuss of Beckham's two early withdrawals against Valencia and Mallorca, this showed he had arrived.

The Daily Telegraph recorded that

> Zinedine Zidane, Raul and Luis Figo are so confident in the new boy's ability that they constantly sought him out with the ball against lively opponents. At one point Zidane and Beckham conducted a series of one-twos together, eliciting roars of 'ole' from Madrid's traditionally demanding fans.

Beckham told those reporters, 'I thought the pace would be slower but it has quickened up; the main difference between here and the Premiership is if you give the ball away it's harder to get it back. This is the happiest I have been for eighteen months.'

More important was winning over the Madrid media. After the next home game, a 7-2 win against Valladolid, in which Beckham played a 50-yard pass for Zidane to volley in, *Marca* spoke of 'a quite fabulous football player'. He even had a puppet on Spain's equivalent of *Spitting Image, Las Noticias del Guinol*. 'We won 7-2 on Saturday and I sold 1,000 shirts,' it boasted. But difficult times lay ahead.

37

Turkey 0 England 0
European Championship Qualifying Group (Istanbul)
11 October 2003

When the draw was made for the 2004 European Championship qualifying groups, the Football Association argued in vain that England should not play Turkey in their final group match, fearing the two meetings between the obvious favourites would be quite tense enough without any possibility of a winner-takes-all contest. Memories of how two Leeds United fans had been killed in Istanbul before a UEFA Cup tie three years earlier, leading to further clashes when Arsenal met Galatasaray in the final, were still fresh in the memory.

Turkey were keen to stage the last game at home, however, and in the inevitable give-and-take of the fixtures meeting, they got their way. The FA's fears were realised in the teams' first contest, at Sunderland in April, when there was crowd trouble before, during and after the game, resulting in the FA being fined £68,000 and a UEFA spokesman warning that England, whose fans had caused problems at Euro 2000, risked being thrown out of the tournament altogether.

In the tunnel afterwards there were threats made by Turkish players and officials, warning of dire reprisals at the return game, which the FA quickly decided they would not allow any English fans to attend. Sven-Goran Eriksson, trying to help matters, had the opposite effect when he prompted fury among the Turks by warning that any who did go to Istanbul risked getting killed, for which he later apologised.

The footballing significance of his team's 2-0 victory at Sunderland, in which Wayne Rooney was outstanding and a hyped-up Beckham was booked and scored the late second goal, was that England eventually went into that second, decisive meeting one point ahead, with only one team automatically qualifying.

Then all the existing tension surrounding the fixture was dramatically added to by the repercussions of Beckham's United teammate Rio Ferdinand failing to attend a routine drugs test. The FA's newish chief executive, Mark Palios, insisted on taking a hard line, telling Eriksson that Ferdinand could not be selected for Istanbul until the matter was resolved, which the Swede did not accept until four days before the game, when his squad was belatedly made public.

The players were furious and at first voted unanimously not to play, thereby forfeiting much of the sympathy for their case. 'Who The Hell Do You Think You Are?' thundered the *Daily Mirror*, above pictures of every member of the squad. It took a phone call from Sir Alex Ferguson to Gary Neville, who had been taking the hardest line of anyone, to persuade him to back off and admit defeat.

Beckham, who as captain had been heavily involved in the discussions, was relieved, but confessed to Neville after a training session described as 'shambolic' that he was seriously concerned about the effect on the team's prospects two days later.

Turkey: Rustu, Uzulmez, Alpay, Korkmaz, Akyel, Emre (Penbe, 79), Buruk (Mansiz, 68), Tugay, Sukur, Nihat, Yalcin (Sanli, 61).
England: James, G Neville, Campbell, Terry, A Cole, Beckham, Butt, Gerrard, Scholes (Lampard, 90), Rooney (Dyer, 73), Heskey (Vassell, 69).
Attendance: 42,000.

Amid one of the most dramatic build-ups in memory to an England game – there had also been well-sourced stories about Eriksson meeting Chelsea to discuss replacing Claudio Ranieri as manager – it was almost a minor detail that Michael Owen would be unable to partner the emerging Rooney in attack because of a shin injury. That meant another start for the willing, if limited Emile Heskey, while John Terry stayed in the side in place of Ferdinand, who had missed the two previous England games anyway.

The atmosphere at the Sukru Saracoglu stadium, Fenerbahce's ground, was as hostile as expected and as England's players bonded together while their national anthem was whistled and booed; the hope was that somehow they would be brought closer together in adversity. So it proved, on an occasion strikingly similar to the goalless draw in Rome that ensured World Cup qualification six years earlier to the exact day.

From subduing Turkey early on, England should have taken the lead with a penalty after 37 minutes. Steven Gerrard was clearly tripped by Tugay, but as Beckham planted his left foot before shooting, it slipped away, causing him to send the ball high over the bar.

Aston Villa's centre-half Alpay responded by going head-to-head with the England captain and in goading him further as the players went down the tunnel at half-time, allegedly making a comment about Beckham's mother; he sparked a brawl involving players on both sides. The two players were summoned into the referee's room for a dressing-down by Pierluigi Collina – him again – but once again the incident had the effect of bringing England together.

Paul Scholes had missed the other two best chances of the first half, while Rooney chipped onto the roof of the net after being put through by Beckham, and in the second half England were once again more dangerous. Beckham actually headed past Rustu Recber with a few minutes to play and although that was disallowed for offside, the defence kept a disappointing Turkey at bay to achieve the desired draw.

David James, given little to do in goal, called it the best defensive performance he had ever played behind and confirmed that the events of the week had unified everyone in the squad.

Alpay admitted afterwards that he had simply been attempting to wind up Beckham, who told reporters, 'It shows people we really are proud to play for our country. After the week beforehand, this was the biggest test this team has had and to come through it, with no fans and everything else, was fantastic.'

'Beck to our best'and 'England regain nation's pride' were the headlines on the front of the *News of the World,* which proclaimed, 'This was the night when every England fan needed to see whether our multi-million pound stars still cared about wearing the national shirt.' Mercifully the answer was 'Yes'.

In *The Guardian* Richard Williams wrote, 'Sven-Goran Eriksson and the rest of the squad threw all the words of disparagement uttered during the week right back in their critics' faces. And the way they chose to do was utterly admirable.'

There was even a small triumph when Eriksson was finally pressed into agreeing that he would definitely be manager of England, not Chelsea or anyone else, at the European finals seven months later. Alas, Rio Ferdinand, hit with an eight-month ban by the FA, would not be there.

38

Barcelona 1 Real Madrid 2
La Liga (Nou Camp)
6 December 2003

From promising beginnings, cracks were occasionally showing at Madrid, which made David Beckham's first *clasico* all the more intense. Although he appeared to have won over those critics who doubted his acquisition, especially when moved to a more central role, the balance of the team was clearly awry.

By the end of September he had played a first Champions League game in the all-white strip, winning plaudits by making a goal for Roberto Carlos in the 4-2 defeat of Marseille. But if a 2-0 defeat at Valencia did not ring alarm bells, losing 4-0 at half-time away to Seville early in November after being torn apart by the former Arsenal winger Jose Antonio Reyes should have done.

Although the final damage was restricted to 4-1, it made the period after the international break that immediately followed a critical one. Beckham, back from Turkey, remained a key figure. As Real narrowly beat lowly Albacete, he gave them a 1-0 lead that lasted barely a minute, and was then named man of the match after curling a free-kick in off the bar in the return Champions League win away to Marseille, and in a 1-1 draw at Osasuna, made the equaliser for Ronaldo when switched in the second half from the right wing to centre-midfield.

There followed a critical week, with his first Madrid derby against Atletico and then a first Barcelona encounter to come, all in the space of four days. Part one went well enough, a 2-0 home win with goals by Ronaldo and Raul, and another triumph for Beckham over his old *bête noire* Diego Simeone; but it was hardly ideal to have only a couple more days to prepare for one of the two biggest fixtures of the season.

Teammates had warned him what to expect in Catalonia. In the previous year's fixture the referee had to order the players off for quarter of an hour to allow everyone to calm down, on and off the pitch. The hated Madrid had not won at the Nou Camp for twenty years in La Liga, only in the European Cup semi-final of 2002 when Steve McManaman cemented his popularity for evermore by scoring in the last minute. Here was a biggest test yet.

Barcelona: Valdés; Gabri (Quaresma, 46), Reiziger, Puyol, Van Bronkhorst, Cocu, Xavi, Motta (Saviola, 77), Gerard, Luis García (Overmars, 46), Kluivert.
Real Madrid: Casillas; Salgado, Raúl Bravo, Pavón, Roberto Carlos, Figo, Helguera, Beckham, Zidane, Raúl (Solari, 85), Ronaldo (Portillo, 76).
Attendance: 98,000

Publicly declaring a preference for joining Real rather than their age-old rivals was always going to be regarded as a heinous offence. The small consolation for Beckham was that in Luis Figo he had a teammate who was loathed in Catalonia for the even worse crime of having walked out on Barcelona to join the Madrid club three years earlier.

So at least the verbal abuse that rained down on the visiting players was shared around. Yet by half-time, the crowd of almost 100,000 had been quietened, and Beckham had played his part. As well as winning a physical midfield battle with the Brazilian Thiago Motta, who at one point caught him with an elbow, Beckham had a hand in the opening goal.

From deep on the right he played a characteristic diagonal pass straight to Zidane on the left wing, who was able to cut back inside and lay the ball off for Roberto Carlos to come steaming in and hit a 25-yard drive that took a useful deflection on its way past Victor Valdes.

Barcelona's coach Frank Rijkaard was sufficiently displeased to make a double change at the interval, replacing Gabri and Luis Garcia with Ricardo Quaresma and Marc Overmars. It improved them but in the 75th minute they fell further behind as Roberto Carlos, with Beckham covering behind him in the left-back position, surged forward and crossed for Ronaldo to take advantage of poor marking and score. Valdes pounded the turf in frustration at having been beaten by another slight deflection, but like the rest of Catalonia he knew it was a long way back now.

Too far; Beckham was among a cluster of defenders unable to prevent Rijkaard's countryman Patrick Kluivert heading in smartly from a corner with a few minutes left but Casillas continued to make saves, including a brave one just before the finish at Kluivert's feet.

At the final whistle Beckham helpfully provided another defining image for the television companies and newspapers by dancing a jig with his friend Roberto Carlos. Understandably carried away by the immensity of the result, he said, 'Coming here as a Madrid player in front of 98,000 and beating Barcelona after all this time is just as sweet as winning the European Cup.'

Coach Carlos Queiroz praised his former Manchester United player by saying,

Every game David takes another step forward. He is gaining knowledge and experience in the middle, maturing. But his commitment, aggression and attitude are always fantastic. David brings intensity, that 90 minutes of complete concentration that characterises English football. Others can learn from his sacrifice.

It was these types of qualities that had endeared him to Madrid supporters as well as his team-mates. Surrounded, he knew, by more naturally gifted players, he had opted to work harder than ever. Simon Talbot, present at the Nou Camp for *The Guardian*, wrote,

> If any last doubts lingered over David Beckham's ability to succeed in Spain they had just been laid to rest in the toughest, most hostile arena. Without him his team-mates insisted that victory over Barcelona would not have been possible. Beckham has settled in record time. The fans are in his pocket, the press is raving, the players consider him fundamental already.
>
> Each year at Madrid is defined by its newcomer. This is Beckham's year; all Madrid's successes this season will forever be defined as his successes.

It just did not seem possible at that time that so little success would be forthcoming.

39

Portugal 2 England 2
(Portugal Won 6-5 on Penalties)
European Championship Quarter-Final (Lisbon)
24 June 2004

By the summer of 2004, playing for England was again a welcome distraction for the team captain, once it came to the actual football. After Real Madrid's ghastly collapse in the last two months of his first season left them fourth in the table and without a trophy, Spain was a good place to escape from, even if he could rarely get away from the spotlight in his own country.

News media picked up on the fact that contrary to expectation, Victoria had never moved to Madrid, causing David to fly back regularly to England. At the squad's pre-tournament media day in June, held at their training based in Sardinia, he initially refused to speak to the English press unless the *Daily Mail* and *News of the World,* which had printed stories and comment about his private life, were excluded. The journalists stuck together, much as England's players had done before the Turkey game, and Beckham relented. But before answering any questions about football, he made a long statement about 'the way the news side have treated me in the last few months', which he described as 'a disgrace'.

Sven-Goran Eriksson, meanwhile, was having his own media problems, having been caught on camera holding talks with Chelsea about taking over as manager from Claudio Ranieri, who was still in the job, the upshot being that he negotiated an extension of his contract for another four years. When the talk came round to the matter in hand, both men's opinions were naturally positive, even though Rio Ferdinand was absent following his long ban.

Talk of a 'golden generation' was growing, and this competition and the next World Cup, both being staged in Europe, were regarded as that generation's best chance of success.

The group stage began dramatically when a strong France side with half a dozen Premier League players came back to beat England 2-1, scoring twice in the last few minutes after Beckham's penalty to give his team a 2-0 lead was saved by Fabien Barthez.

Eriksson, concerned that Beckham, Steven Gerrard, Frank Lampard and Paul Scholes all wanted to play centrally, consulted his senior players about the diamond midfield formation, which was dropped, leading to inevitable press comment about 'player power'. That gave way to what *The Sun*'s front page labelled 'Rooney-mania' after the young Evertonian, emerging as a genuine international star, destroyed Switzerland and then Croatia to earn a quarter-final place against Portugal in Lisbon.

Beckham had not been at his best and like everyone else he would need to be against opponents regarded as beatable but claiming all the natural advantages accruing to a host country.

Portugal: Ricardo, Miguel (Rui Costa, 79), Andrade, Ricardo Carvalho, Nuno Valente, Maniche, Costinha (Simao, 63), Deco, Figo (Postiga, 75), Nuno Gomes, Ronaldo.
England: James, G. Neville, Terry, Campbell, A. Cole, Beckham, Lampard, Gerrard (Hargreaves, 81), Scholes (P. Neville, 57), Owen, Rooney, (Vassell, 27).
Attendance: 65,000.

The start could hardly have been better, although the mood among England's thousands of supporters in the *Estadio da Luz* was checked within half an hour. In the 3rd minute they were celebrating wildly as Costinha failed to cut out David James' long kick downfield, which was pounced upon by Michael Owen, flicking it deftly past Ricardo. It was the fourth successive tournament in which he had scored – a new national record.

A devastating blow followed when Rooney, who had come to embody all England's hopes, went down with what turned out to be a fractured metatarsal. Darius Vassell, his replacement, was a trier and a team player, but not remotely in the same class.

As the pressure built up, Eriksson made two defensive substitutions, taking off Scholes, who was again suffering in the heat, and Gerrard, who the manager said had cramp, and with Sol Campbell and Ashley Cole outstanding in defence his team had to hold out for only 7 minutes more when a substitution by Luiz Felipe Scolari paid off best. England had been perfectly happy to see the back of Luis Figo, but it was his replacement, the little regarded Tottenham striker Helder Postiga (two goals in twenty-four games) who struck by heading in a cross from another sub, Simao.

Although the host country were well on top at that stage there was a critical incident just before the end of normal time, when Campbell thought he had scored a winning goal following Beckham's free-kick. Just like the Argentina game in 1998, he was dismayed to see it disallowed for a push by a team-mate, in this case John Terry.

With three changes already made by each side, fatigue weighed heavily on both in extra-time, contributing if anything to the drama. After Cole cleared from the goal line, Rui Costa appeared to have put Portugal into the semi-final with a fierce shot from 20 yards, only for Lampard to swivel and equalise as Terry headed down a Beckham corner.

So penalties it was – never an outcome to inspire confidence in English supporters or perhaps even their players. This time, watched by a peak television audience of 24.7 million, they would score more than normal in a controversial shoot-out but still not win.

Beckham, having missed his last two, stepped up first but was furious to see the turf on the penalty spot scuff up as his shot sailed high over the bar.

With nerves fraying, Owen and Lampard were a little fortunate to score with unconvincing kicks down the centre, but when Rui Costa followed Beckham in shooting too high and glaring at the penalty spot, they were back on level terms and then able to lead 3-2, 4-3 and 5-4 thanks to Terry, Hargreaves – who got away with moving the ball off the sandiest spot – and Cole.

Were England to win a shoot-out at last? They would have done if James had stood still for Postiga's chip straight down the middle. Instead he moved and it went in. Ricardo then made himself the hero of all Portugal by saving well from Vassell and confidently striding up himself to beat James just inside a post for the winning kick.

In the immediate aftermath the talk was naturally about penalties. Beckham, whose worst enemy could hardly accuse him of being bad at set-pieces, insisted that as in Turkey, he had been betrayed by the pitch:

> We actually practised our penalties at the other end and our feet were giving way with every kick we took. The manager made a complaint to UEFA, who said they would repair it but I don't think they did. It wasn't just me. The other lads complained that the turf was moving when they kicked the ball. I have watched my penalty on television and when I plant my left foot to take the kick you can see the ball lift up. I could not have hit the ball that way normally if I tried.

The *Daily Mail,* which had pondered the previous day 'why David Beckham has been the big disappointment of Euro 2004', gave him a respectable 6/10 and commented that he was 'much more involved. Delivered effective crosses. Solid in helping Neville.' The injury to Rooney, meanwhile, was lamented as 'one of sport's most terrible injustices' for 'the teenage terror who had lit up the entire carnival'.

UEFA dismissed Beckham's complaint, their communications director William Gaillard saying, 'Everyone was looking at the penalty spots before taking the kicks. It seems that one player had a particular problem with the penalty spot but none of the others.' Rui Costa, Hargreaves and probably others too could have told him that was untrue.

When the debate widened to broader issues, the *Mail's* Jeff Powell, never a fan of either England's manager or captain, asked if the 'love affair' between the two was over, criticised 'celebrity soccer gone mad' and asked of Beckham:

> How much was he drained by his marital tribulations and his constant commuting from Spain to Beckingham Palace? Instead of crying over slipped penalties, England should be concerned at the way they were outclassed. They would have been massacred in 90 minutes if Portugal had a cutting edge striker or two.

In the last post-mortem, Beckham, 'defiant and defensive at times, visibly deflated at others', said he saw no reason to resign the captaincy, defended his commercial involvement and added, 'I don't believe the criticism is fair. I haven't put in as many crosses as I normally do but I've been playing a different way. I can still look at myself in the mirror and know I've given 100 per cent.

40

Portugal 0 England 0
(Portugal Won 3-1 on Penalties)
World Cup (Gelsenkirchen)
1 July 2006

It is perhaps unsurprising if, some years after the events, the quarter-finals of 2004 and 2006 tend to merge into one in the memory: Sven-Goran Eriksson against Luiz Felipe Scolari, a familiar cast of heroes and villains, one or key absentees, English injuries and of course penalties.

At the end of it all, reaction was not too different either, except for a weary acceptance that now Eriksson's 'golden generation' really had run its course and that the gold was a rather baser metal. For David Beckham, criticised even more heavily than before, it would all end in tears – literally and metaphorically.

England's qualification for the tournament was again fraught, after a first defeat by Northern Ireland in nineteen meetings once more coming down to the last match to avoid the play-offs, which was achieved when Poland were beaten 2-1 at Old Trafford.

Eriksson, told he would not be retained after the finals, caused a sensation by naming the seventeen-year-old Theo Walcott in his squad as one of only four strikers. He also had to fight Manchester United for the right to pick another of them, Wayne Rooney, who the club insisted would not be fit after breaking a metatarsal at Stamford Bridge late in April.

Once in Germany, the other key striker, Michael Owen, damaged knee ligaments in the final group match against Sweden. England, unconvincing in wins over against Paraguay and Trinidad & Tobago, then stumbled past Ecuador 1-0 thanks to Beckham's 30-yard free-kick. It made him the first England player to score at three World Cups and earned a repeat encounter against Portugal two years on from Lisbon.

England: Robinson, G. Neville, Terry, Ferdinand, A. Cole, Hargreaves, Beckham (Lennon, 51, Carragher, 118), Gerrard, Lampard, J. Cole (Crouch, 65), Rooney.
Portugal: Ricardo, Miguel, Meira, Ricardo Carvalho, Nuno Valente, Figo (Postiga, 86), Maniche, Petit, Tiago (Viana, 74), Ronaldo, Pauleta (Simao, 63).
Attendance: 52,000.

Not only were the two managers the same, but each team fielded seven players from the previous game. It could have been nine for Portugal, had Deco and Costinha not been suspended for two of the four red cards handed out in a wild second round win over Holland, and eight for England had Owen been fit.

In his absence, Eriksson again used five midfielders, hoping that Lampard and Gerrard would support Rooney while Beckham and Joe Cole supplied the width and Owen Hargreaves protected the defence. The conservative formation led to an uneventful first half under the roof at the AufSchalke Stadium, in which Paul Robinson nevertheless had to save from Cristiano Ronaldo, Pauleta and Petit.

Beckham, having a quiet game after supplying crucial assists and a goal in the earlier matches, had strong penalty appeals for handball by Nuno Valente from one of his crosses turned down, and early in the second half reluctantly agreed he could no longer continue because of a torn ankle tendon.

If anything his replacement Aaron Lennon livened England up, despite the shock of losing Rooney only 10 minutes later. However much his frustration as an isolated lone attacker was getting to him, there was no excuse for the United player's lunge that caught Ricardo Carvalho between the legs. Whether malicious or merely careless, it meant a red card that condemned his teammates to toil through the rest of the game a man short.

In the end, that would mean a whole hour, since regulation time did not produce a goal. Peter Crouch was brought on for Joe Cole almost as soon as Rooney was sent off; Figo and Hugo Viana went closest for Portugal – Lampard with a free-kick and Lennon from the follow-up for England.

In extra-time fatigue kicked in and although the tension heightened, penalties were always a strong possibility, so much so that Eriksson took off one substitute, Lennon, and replaced him with another, Jamie Carragher, because the Liverpool defender had been so impressive with penalty kicks in training.

England had practised them regularly, including the lonely walk from the halfway line. By the time it came to the real thing, of course, neither Beckham, Rooney nor Owen were available. Unlike Lisbon, Portugal had the advantage of going first, although they seemed equally edgy. Four of the first six kicks were missed, by Lampard, Viana, Petit and Gerrard; only Simao and Hargreaves (voted man of the match) were successful.

Helder Postiga put Portugal 2-1 ahead and although Carragher scored, the referee ordered a re-take, which Ricardo saved. Ronaldo, who would gain notoriety for his wink after Rooney's dismissal, then stepped forward and beat Robinson to take Portugal into the semi-final (which they lost 1-0 to France).

Scolari, who would soon become the main target as Eriksson's successor, praised the 'incredible' way England had fought with ten men, but there was far less sympathy from their compatriots, above all in the media.

Beckham was awarded a mark of five out of ten in *The Observer*, which commented:

Ended his afternoon weeping following the injury that removed him. Had been largely anonymous. Eriksson's man on the pitch through his five-year reign owed his head coach more and when Lennon came on the feeling was the side's chances improved.

The following day Beckham was again fighting to hold back the tears as he announced his resignation from the captaincy in a prepared statement:

> This decision has been the most difficult of my career to date but after discussing it with my family and those closest to me I feel the time is right. Our performances during this World Cup have not been enough to progress further and both myself and all the players regret that and are hurt by that more than people realise.

Criticised two years earlier for not resigning, he was now harangued in some quarters for doing so, instead of waiting to be sacked. Eriksson was more reasonably berated for the dullness of England's football and the mistake of taking Walcott instead of another experienced striker, who could have come in for Owen. Howard Wilkinson had a good line: 'We went to Germany with a team of stars, not a star team.'

Meanwhile those who had lambasted the manager and captain two years earlier, and for some time beforehand, were hardly going to recant. James Lawton, chief sportswriter of *The Independent,* lamented Eriksson's 'disgraceful stewardship' and wrote of Beckham,

> In all his appearances in three World Cups and two European Championships his influence and his impact have been negligible. The manner of his resignation summed up all that has been wrong with the Eriksson-Beckham regime. The captaincy of England is a rare and precious gift and should be received and returned at the bidding of the man in charge – the coach of the team.

In the same paper, Sam Wallace's verdict was rather more restrained:

> The regime did not implode or collapse dramatically, it just faded in that inauspicious style peculiar to Eriksson's England teams. The numbing defeat by penalties is an English tradition but it was also a fittingly pointless way for Eriksson to go.

His judgment on Beckham could hardly be disputed: 'An emotional man, whose life unfolds in a series of triumphs and disasters'. Even at the age of thirty-one, there were more to come.

41

England 1 Brazil 1
Friendly (Wembley)
1 June 2007

Steve McClaren, promoted to become Sven-Goran Eriksson's successor after Luiz Felipe Scolari declined the opportunity, made some big decisions in his first couple of months in the job. One was to appoint Terry Venables as his assistant, the next was to make John Terry England's captain and the third was to drop David Beckham. He told an inaugural press conference,

David's reaction was exactly the one I expected. He's got pride and was disappointed but said he understood and wanted to fight for his place. He's got to do what he said he would do – perform as best he can at Real Madrid and hope the door is open enough.

Left out of the Madrid team as well later in the season, because manager Fabio Capello felt he would be insufficiently motivated after having agreed to join LA Galaxy, Beckham's typical reaction was to get his head down and win a place back, which he eventually did for both club and country.

Thus when Wembley staged a first England game since October 2000, a glamorous fixture against Brazil, the name of Beckham was not only on the squad list but on the back of the familiar number 7 shirt to earn a ninety-fifth cap. Stewart Downing, Aaron Lennon and Shaun Wright-Phillips had all failed to make that shirt their own since the World Cup and McClaren admitted that after four games without a win from October to February, he would have recalled Beckham for the two March fixtures but for injury.

Deciding to do so with a crucial European Championship qualifying game away to Estonia coming five days after the Brazil game brought the Beckham critics out in force and forced the manager to declare,

It is certainly not a panic move. After the Spain game in February, we reassessed things and looked at changing things round and David came into the reckoning. I made plans to go out and watch him with a view to bringing him in for the Israel and Andorra matches but he got a knee injury. I met him ten days ago and we had a chat about the possibility of him coming back and he is still passionate about playing for his country.

England: Robinson, Carragher, Terry (Brown, 72), King, Shorey, Beckham (Jenas, 77), Gerrard, Lampard (Carrick, 88), J. Cole (Downing, 62), Smith (Dyer, 62), Owen (Crouch, 83).

Brazil: Helton, Dani Alves (Maicon, 65), Naldo, Juan, Gilberto, Mineiro (Edmilson, 63), Gilberto Silva, Kaka (Alves, 71), Ronaldinho, Robinho (Diego, 74), Vagner Love.

Attendance: 88,745.

The decision to spend almost £800 million revamping Wembley had divided opinion just as much as the former captain's recall, but there was a good atmosphere on a balmy June evening, diluted a little once Brazil established their superiority in the first half.

Gilberto Silva was unfortunate to have a headed goal disallowed when it was Vagner Love, not the Arsenal player, who was in an offside position. Meanwhile Ronaldinho and Robinho often troubled Terry and his fellow defenders, who included Reading's Nicky Shorey on a debut at left-back.

Early in the second half, Paul Robinson was required to make a good save from Ronaldinho before England produced some pressure of their own, with Beckham prominent. Having clipped one free-kick wide in the first half, he supplied another for Michael Owen – also playing a first England game since the World Cup – to head onto the roof of the net.

Downing, on as a substitute for Joe Cole on the left flank, had a fierce 30-yard drive touched over the bar and then, in the 68th minute, Wembley saw its first England goal in exactly seven years. Beckham took another free-kick from the right, placing it this time beyond the far post, where Terry played the captain's part by outjumping the lanky Naldo to head past Helton.

Terry picked up an injury in the process and when his replacement Wes Brown slipped over, England were lucky that Afonso Alves shot wide. He should have scored too after Naldo headed on Ronaldinho's corner. That was just after Beckham was withdrawn, receiving a standing ovation from all round the ground.

Peter Crouch came on, too late to benefit from Beckham's crosses, and just before the finish Brazil claimed a deserved equaliser. Midfielder Diego was allowed too much space in the penalty area and headed in Gilberto Silva's cross.

Gerrard was named official man of the match, but Beckham was star man in *The Sun*, whose ratings said, 'England's prodigal son played a great early ball to Owen before flashing a trademark free-kick wide. Was our most creative player, delivered a superb ball for Terry to head home. 8/10.'

The main headline read, 'It's Beck to the future' and Shaun Custis wrote,

All those who doubted David Beckham, go to the back of the class – and collect your dunce's hats on the way. Yes, Terry Venables, that includes you.

England's assistant manager was against a recall for the country's former skipper. But Steve McClaren, who axed Becks after the World Cup, swallowed his pride and was totally vindicated.

Terry, grateful for the assist for his goal, said, 'David was different class, his delivery was superb.' Touched by his ovation when substituted, Beckham added,

It's nice to know I still have the support of the fans. I've had their backing throughout my career but tonight was just amazing. I'm not sure which was louder, the reception I got before the game or when I came off. I enjoyed being part of such an historic occasion for the whole country at the new Wembley – and it's great to be back. Whether I thought I'd ever play for England again doesn't matter now. Hopefully I've done enough to keep my place against Estonia.

So he did, when a 3-0 away win included two more Beckham assists, relieving the pressure on McClaren and putting England's campaign back on track. Long before the vital autumn games against Russia and Croatia, however, there was a first La Liga title to secure.

42

Real Madrid 3 Real Mallorca 1
La Liga (Bernabeu Stadium)
17 June 2007

Had David Beckham been told on 17 June 2003, the day Real Madrid signed him, that four years later he would have won nothing other than one Spanish Super Cup (the equivalent of the Community Shield), he would have suspected some sort of joke. The only question on his arrival appeared to be how to fit all the superstars, the *galaticos,* into one team. Perhaps that was the problem.

In three seasons Madrid finished fourth, second and second in La Liga, behind Barcelona every time. Each Champions League campaign ended in failure too, the combination of which led to a string of managers coming and going. Carlos Queiroz was followed by Jose Antonio Camacho, then Mariano Garcio Remon, Vanderlei Luxemburgo and Juan Lopez Caro, not one of whom lasted more than a full year.

In 2006, even the president, Florentino Perez, resigned. His successor Ramon Calderon delayed sorting out a new contract for Beckham, who in January 2007 took up what had become the increasingly attractive option to join the LA Galaxy that summer. Fabio Capello had been brought in by Calderon and given £75 million to sign eight new players, including Ruud van Nistelrooy but despite the latter's goals, Real still lagged behind Barca in the league.

Told of Beckham's plans, Calderon said he was about to become 'a half -baked actor living in Hollywood' and Capello decreed he would no longer be picked - only to relent a month later. On 10 February he returned to the side and scored the equaliser from a 30-yard free-kick in a narrow victory over Real Sociedad. After an epic 3-3 draw at Barcelona on 10 March, a few days after going out of the Champions League to Bayern Munich, Madrid were still in fourth place with a dozen games to play, but nine of the next ten were won and suddenly, if unexpectedly, the title was in sight.

Capello's side regularly rescued vital points in the last few minutes of games and going into the final day they were level on points with Barcelona. The free-scoring Catalans had much the better goal-difference, but in Spain it was the head-to-head results that were crucial, and Real had the advantage by virtue of having won their home game 2-0 back in October, then drawing at the Nou Camp.

All they needed to do was match Barcelona's result against Gimnastic on the final day to win back the title at last. But even that was not straightforward.

Real Madrid: Casillas, Salgado, Ramos, Cannavaro, Roberto Carlos, Beckham (Reyes, 65), Emerson (Guti, 46), Diarra, Robinho, Raul, Van Nistelrooy (Higuain, 32)
Real Mallorca: Moya, Hector, Ballesteros, Nunes (Ramis, 35), Navarro, Varela, Basinas, Pereyra, Jonas, Victor (Maxi Lopez, 67), Arango.
Attendance: 80,000.

The capacity crowd, having arrived for a coronation, were kept in a state of high tension for almost the whole game. Mallorca, sitting in the middle of the table, had reportedly been offered a bonus by a Barcelona businessman to deny Madrid victory and whether financial incentives or relaxed end-of-term mood were the decisive factor, everything seemed to be going their way – and therefore Barcelona's.

In the very first minute the visitors' striker Juan Arango drove a shot against the post, and just after the quarter-hour, the same player fed Fernando Varela to open the scoring.

As Van Nistelrooy, Madrid's top scorer, limped off with an ankle injury, concern deepened and by half-time news was buzzing round the stadium that Barca led 3-0 against bottom-of-the-table Gimnastic.

Beckham, willed on in what everyone now knew would be his last game, put one free-kick on top of the net, and another against the angle of bar and post. After 65 minutes, however, soon after Varela had missed an excellent chance to make it 2-0, he too was forced off. The ovation from a nervous crowd was sympathetic rather than rapturous one that might have been expected if Real had been ahead. Yet it turned out that his replacement, Jose Antonio Reyes, scourge of Madrid in Beckham's first season, was to prove a saviour.

Only a few minutes after coming on Reyes turned in the equaliser from 6 yards out. Another goal was still required and in the 79th minute, a header by Mahamadou Diarra, rushed back from international duty with Mali, hit the goalkeeper Miguel Angel Moya, then defender Angelos Basinas and crept over the line.

Given the regular catastrophes over the past four seasons, there was still every chance of a fallible defence slipping up, until Reyes curled in a fine left-footed drive from well outside the penalty area and the title was finally assured.

Instead of a horrible anticlimax, Beckham, draped in a Union flag and with a bandaged knee and injured ankle, was able to celebrate on the pitch with his team-mates at last while Victoria and his friend Tom Cruise exulted in from the main stand.

'Fairy-tale farewell,' headlined the *Daily Mail,* reporting,

Dismissed as a mannequin when he first arrived at the Bernabeu four years ago, David Beckham departed last night in the manner he always said he would. As a much admired midfielder with a precious La Liga medal to show for his considerable efforts.

If this was the hardest season of a long and eventful career, it ended on an incredible high for the former England captain. Not only with the promise of more caps from Steve McClaren but with the satisfaction that comes with proving a point.

It was hardly the first time he had done that. So impressed were Capello and the Madrid hierarchy that they immediately tried to undo his transfer to LA Galaxy, who were understandably having none of it.

The club and Major League Soccer had invested too much time, faith and money in what journalist Grant Wahl's book would call *The Beckham Experiment* to pull back now.

43

LA Galaxy 0 Chelsea 1
Friendly (Home Depot Center)
21 July 2007

As one of the most recognisable sportsmen in the world, David Beckham had long been coveted by Major League Soccer and in particular by the Anschutz Entertainment Group, which at one time had an interest in six of the ten MLS teams. The parties had been brought together as early as 2002, leading to discussions about backing Beckham soccer academies in London and Los Angeles, and during his time at Real Madrid there were regular business and social get-togethers.

Victoria, significantly, was much keener on going to LA than she had been on moving to Madrid and once Real hesitated about a new contract in 2006, the time suddenly seemed right. The Galaxy, like Madrid, were much more aware of Beckham's commercial potential than Manchester United had ever been; so much so that Ivan Gazidis, deputy commissioner of MLS at the time, and later chief executive of Arsenal, was able to claim of the five-year contract worth $32.5million : 'It was a great deal for MLS and also for the Galaxy. On the day we signed him most of the money had already been recouped.'

European observers with a dim view of football in America naturally felt he had given up any serious pretension of remaining a top player. 'How can you leave Real Madrid for LA Galaxy?' Sir Alex Ferguson wondered. Yet for personal, family, social and - not least - financial reasons, it was a brilliant move.

A friendly against Chelsea, who under Jose Mourinho found the US ideal for pre-season preparation, should have been a perfect start: it was being called 'the most publicised game in MLS history'. ESPN had been running whole programmes devoted to Beckham in the build-up, and lined up live coverage of the match with nineteen cameras, one of which would be trained on the star attraction from start to finish, and another on celebrities in the crowd. There was only one problem: Beckham's injured left ankle.

Not since his broken metatarsal before the World Cup had there been so much attention on a Beckham injury. The ankle had been sprained in England's final match of the season away to Estonia, forcing him off 20 minutes from the end. Desperate not to miss Real Madrid's last two crucial games in the following fortnight, he had pain-killing injections, played in both and did further damage to the ligaments.

A long period of rest and treatment was ideally required. Instead he was needed within five weeks for his heavily promoted Galaxy debut, and two days beforehand was telling reporters 'it doesn't look that I'm going to play'. Club officials and television executives were soon putting a much more positive spin on things and it soon became clear that whatever it took, David Beckham would be out on the pitch at some stage on the evening of 21 July.

LA Galaxy: Cannon, Harden, Jazic, Roberts, Xavier, Martino (Glinton, 72), Pavon (Vagenas, 61), Gordon (Beckham, 78), Donovan, Jones (Kirk, 56), Gray.
Chelsea: Cech (Cudicini, 46), Essien, Terry, Carvalho, Ferreira (J.Cole, 46), Wright-Phillips (Shevchenko, 46), Lampard (Sidwell, 74), Ben Haim (Mikel, 46), Malouda (Johnson, 74), Drogba (Hutchinson, 89), Kalou (Makelele, 61).
Attendance: 27,000.

The injury doubts only added to the drama of the event. However dull the match might have been – which, like many such friendlies, it essentially was – for over an hour, the capacity crowd of 27,000 (up 42 per cent on the 2006 average) were able to console themselves that the 'I was there' moment was still to come.

The Galaxy team were not in great shape, second bottom of the MLS table with three wins out of twelve, which put their coach Frank Yallop, once of Ipswich Town, under further pressure. In the first half against a rusty Chelsea, however, those home fans studying the game as opposed to the home bench had some cause for encouragement as Petr Cech was forced to save from Cobi Jones and Abel Xavier. Florent Malouda and Salomon Kalou wasted chances for Chelsea, who then made four changes at half-time and took the lead early in the second half with a goal by John Terry, set up by Joe Cole.

There were six further substitutions before the one that the home crowd wanted to see finally materialised. *The Daily Telegraph's* Oliver Brown, one of a large British press contingent, described it thus:

> The stars were in perfect alignment as David Beckham made an entrance of cosmic impact. He had waited 78 minutes and when he rose from the bench to a peal of rapturous acclaim, he gave the sense that this game they call soccer would never be the quite the same again.
>
> So deliriously did the crowd react it was as if a large firework had just been detonated – there was the same thunderclap of noise, the same frantic flicker of light as Beckham was framed by a thousand camera flashes.

In twelve remaining minutes, he touched the ball only eight times but according to the Reuters report, 'helped steady the midfield with a polished cameo performance'. One classic 40-yard pass had the crowd in raptures before an anxious moment right at the end when Chelsea substitute Steve Sidwell, a vigorous midfielder playing for his place among a crop of international stars, clattered into Beckham and brought him down.

Despite further damage to the ankle, he was able to continue until the final whistle and later made the right noises amid all his media duties:

> I was proud of the way people reacted to me. The reaction when I took my top off or kicked the ball was incredible. It makes me feel a little embarrassed sometimes. But to have a full stadium as we did here was a credit to the people of LA who have supported the MLS for so many years. It was very emotional. You don't get that kind of atmosphere directed towards one person often. This last week had truly been one of the most remarkable of my life. The attention has been immense – not just on the Galaxy but on me, [and] on my family. It has all been positive and I hope that continues.

Mourinho – who, astonishingly, would leave Chelsea within two months – was generous about the opposition and Beckham's prospects as a missionary:

> LA played the game with a lot of passion, I think maybe they wanted to show David Beckham they have a team. They were highly motivated and they gave us a hard game. I think this is the correct attitude to play football. If they continue doing this, they will get results and they will improve. For those players who are not of a high level, playing with Beckham at their side in sold-out stadiums with a great atmosphere must be a motivation. I imagine it will be very easy for him to help Americans fall in love with the game.

Television ratings of 947,000, five times the average MLS audience, were still regarded as a disappointment, although Beckham made at least one influential convert. The *Los Angeles Times* headlined 'Start of something big' and sportswriter Bill Plaschke summed up the combination of cynicism and reluctant admiration that surrounded much of the Englishman's foreign travels:

> It was a publicity stunt. It was a human billboard. It was vaudeville ... as phoney as his wife's television debut. Then why can't I stop smiling? I was the guy who was bored by Beckham, remember? What's really crazy is I'm not bored anymore. Turns out, even on a bum ankle, David Beckham is a blast.

44

New York Red Bulls 5 LA Galaxy 4
MLS (Giants Stadium)
18 August 2007

In order to maximise Beckham's impact, the Galaxy had been given a schedule for the second half of their season that even someone accustomed to English football would have found daunting: it basically involved two games a week, but with including thousands of miles of travelling to and from away matches.

Reaching the final of the Superliga (an eight-team competition played between US and Mexican clubs) meant that from 24 July to 1 September inclusive they played twelve games, but to everyone's frustration the ankle problems exacerbated by Chelsea's Steve Sidwell meant Beckham was able to take part for only 13 minutes altogether in the first six of them.

He sat out the extraordinary 6-5 Superliga win over Dallas, came on as a late substitute in a 1-0 away defeat by DC United (watched by England manager Steve McClaren) and finally started for the first time at home to the same opposition in the Superliga semi-final in mid-August. Having taken the captaincy from a slightly miffed Landon Donovan, Beckham played a leader's role in scoring from a trademark free-kick and making the second goal for Donovan in a victory that earned a place in the final against Pachuca of Mexico.

Only three days later the Galaxy flew to New York for a match that Beckham would say took him back to his childhood for its end-to-end play, goals and excitement. Fittingly, given the drama to come, his presence helped draw a crowd of more than 66,000 to it – six times the Red Bulls' average and a record for a regular season MLS game.

New York Red Bulls: Waterreus, Freeman, Parke, Stammler, Leitch, Richards, Mathis (Mendes, 90) Vide, Van den Bergh (Wolyniec, 84), Altidore (Magee, 90), Angel.
LA Galaxy: Cannon, Klein, Harden, Jazic (Glinton, 17),(Buddle, 76), Randolph, Beckham, Donovan, Harmse, Martino, Pavon, Gordon (Veris, 60).
Attendance: 66,237.

Not surprisingly, Beckham's MLS travels often brought him across old adversaries from English or Spanish football. In New York there was one in the shape of Juan Pablo Angel, the Colombian striker who had signed from Aston Villa that season, and was to have the first and last word in a sensational game.

Lining up alongside a less successful Premier League player of the future, the seventeen-year-old Jozy Altidore, Angel started the scoring in only the fourth minute, driving a free-kick low through the Galaxy wall. The Los Angeles side's response belied their recent form and helped convince any doubters that this guy Beckham might have something to offer after all. By the 9th minute, he had placed a corner on Carlos Pavon's head for the equaliser and then had done the same with a free-kick from out on the right: 2-1 to the visitors.

'Beckham has brought a level of danger to the Galaxy attack that has been missing for, oh, about 11 years,' posted one live blogger. 'Something good seems to happen each time he gets his foot on the ball.'

His next free-kick from a similar position led to a header by Alan Gordon that Dutch goalkeeper Ronald Waterreus had to kick away with his feet, but after the Galaxy's Mike Randolph cleared off the line from Jeff Parke, the Red Bulls came back with a volleyed equaliser right on half-time from Clint Mathis .

Early in the second half the home side were back in front through the precocious Altidore, whose next goal after 71 minutes was immediately followed by a reply from Donovan: 4-3. With his ankle now playing up painfully on the artificial pitch, Beckham continued to strike a series of free-kicks and corners that came to nothing until the 82nd minute, when one of the latter was met by one Galaxy substitute, Kyle Veris, and jabbed in by another, Edson Buddle, as it came back off the crossbar: 4-4.

The comeback, alas, was to be in vain. With just a couple of minutes to play, Cannon could only push out a 30-yard drive by Mathis and Angel turned it past him from an acute angle for the winning goal.

The crowd rose in appreciation of both sides' efforts and were applauded in turn by Beckham (who had been booed throughout). 'Every ball he touched was a piece of magic,' Angel said admiringly.

'I was surprised to actually play 90 minutes,' Beckham added. 'My ankle took quite a bit of pounding on the turf. It's a surface I'm not used to.'

Delighted MLS commissioner Don Garber described it as 'one of the best sports experiences I've ever attended' – contrasting it favourably with his numerous Super Bowl finals.

The downside was the pressure heaped on Beckham and the Galaxy for more of the same. So after heading straight back to London for England's friendly against Germany, and playing another 90 minutes, he felt obliged to declare himself fit for at least half of the club's televised home game with Chivas USA the very next day. He ended up playing the whole match for the third time in six days and finished it exhausted and barely able to move as boos rained down amid a 3-0 defeat.

A week later he badly injured a knee in the first half of the Superliga final, (which the Galaxy lost on penalties), and missed all but the last of the remaining games. Despite winning five successive matches without him, when Landon Donovan said the players felt far more relaxed, the club finished only fifth out of six in the Western Conference, whereupon an overwhelmed Yallop resigned before he was pushed.

Beckham had played only 352 minutes of a possible 2,000-plus. As with the New York game, his initial contributions had hugely increased interest, publicity and attendances, but under pressure to justify himself he had come back from injury too soon, played on instead of resting and paid the price.

Asked on the CBS news programme *60 Minutes* to sum up his first season, he replied frankly 'a nightmare'.

45

England 3 Belarus 0
World Cup Qualifying Group (Wembley)
14 October 2009

Having praised David Beckham for proving himself 'a great man and great player' during their time together at Real Madrid, England's new manager, Fabio Capello, called him up for a 100th cap away to France in March 2008 (the Italian's second match). He took the captain's armband for what would prove to be the last time three months later in Trinidad & Tobago, and during the 2010 World Cup qualifying campaign was used mostly as a substitute, starting only the 6-0 win over Andorra in June 2009.

By the following autumn, he found himself in the squad but playing no part in two of the three games; when England lost 1-0 in Ukraine after goalkeeper Rob Green was sent off early on, it was the first time in memory Beckham had been in the squad but was not even an unused substitute. Capello correctly said he had no more right to a place than anyone else, and with the team safely qualified after winning their first eight matches, the manager was thinking ahead to the finals in South Africa: Theo Walcott, Shaun Wright-Phillips, Ashley Young and Aaron Lennon, as well as the versatile James Milner, were all in contention for the wide places.

Come the following Wednesday, however, there was to be one more hurrah for the country's most capped outfield player.

England: Foster, Johnson, Ferdinand, Terry, Bridge (Milner, 78), Lennon (Beckham, 58), Lampard, Barry, Wright-Phillips, Crouch, Agbonlahor (C. Cole, 66).
Belarus: Zhevnov, Kulchy, Yurevich, Sosnovskiy, Bordachev (Kashevsky, 84), Verkhovtsov, Omelyanchuk, Shitov, Kalachev, Kornilenko (Kovel, 77), Kutuzov (Rodionov, 45).
Attendance: 76,897.

Lennon and Wright-Phillips started the game as Capello went for two out-and-out wingers on either side of Frank Lampard and Gareth Barry to service Peter Crouch. Steven Gerrard, Wayne Rooney and David James were all missing, allowing Ben Foster a start in goal.

Having beaten Croatia 5-1 a month earlier, England were not expected to have much trouble with Belarus, and a similar result seemed on the cards when they took the lead in only the fourth minute. Gabriel Agbonlahor, sent through by Barry, laid on a cross for Crouch to bundle in from a few yards out.

After that the visitors, packing midfield against Lampard and Barry, held out more comfortably than Capello would have liked and he confessed to being angry at half-time. That no doubt influenced the decision to replace Lennon just before the hour with Beckham, who immediately played a short corner straight to Wright-Phillips, the Manchester City player shifting the ball to his right and driving it into the net.

Foster, winning his third cap, made one good save from Sergei Omelyanchuk before Crouch scored his second close-range goal a quarter of an hour from the end, this time after following in a shot by substitute Carlton Cole. Milner, taking his versatility to the limit by operating at left-back, hit a post and so did Beckham, denied what would have been his eighteenth goal from 115 appearances. Although no one knew it at the time, it proved to be his last significant contribution as an England player.

He had livened England up on the night and impressed with his passing and crossing. There was still widespread disbelief when the Sunderland manager Steve Bruce named him ITV's man of the match, having joked that he could not give it to Crouch after the lanky striker turned down a move to Sunderland that summer.

As Sam Wallace wrote in *The Independent*,

> In his pundit's suit Bruce was not the only one who came over all giddy at the sight of Beckham. Giving him the man of the match award for 32 minutes was ludicrous but the adoring thousands at Wembley did not care ...
>
> Like Crouch, Beckham is another player who cannot be certain of his place in the squad come next summer and, like Crouch, he is one of those who offers England something different. But it remains to be seen whether he fits into Capello's masterplan.

In the meantime, desperate to be under consideration, Beckham announced after the game that returning to AC Milan, where he had spent the previous American off-season, was '95 per cent certain'. Capello was all in favour, saying,

> It's very important because Beckham when he played the last 20 minutes or half an hour, he's always played very well and been focused. Sometimes some players when they're substitutes have problems playing normally. Beckham always plays well.

Even the manager admitted to being surprised at the man of the match nomination, caustically describing it as 'like Obama getting the Nobel Peace Prize after eight months as president' (which had happened five days earlier). He did, however, select Beckham again for the friendly at home to Egypt in March, without bringing him off the substitutes' bench, suggesting he was very much in World Cup contention.

Later that month Milan played at Manchester United in the Champions League (see Chapter 47), but in their next game, against Chievo Verona, he tore an Achilles tendon and was out of the World Cup and all football for five months. Capello picked Lennon and Wright-Phillips for South Africa, but ended up using Milner and Steven Gerrard in the last two matches of a shocking campaign there, which suggested Beckham, who travelled with the squad as 'player liaison man' could have been of some use as an occasional substitute were it not for the injury.

At the first international of the following season against Hungary, the manager announced he did not intend picking Beckham for any more competitive games, but hoped he might appear in one more Wembley friendly 'so the fans can say goodbye'. It did not happen.

46

LA Galaxy 1 Real Salt Lake 1
(Real won 5-4 on Penalties)
MLS Cup Final (Qwest Field, Seattle)
22 November 2009

Just as with Real Madrid, David Beckham's career in the United States was to finish much better than it started. It was again a long haul, however. If his first season (more precisely, a half-season, ending in October 2007), was a self-confessed 'nightmare' the second was not much of an improvement.

In 2008, the Galaxy finished seventh out of eight teams, after Ruud Gullit, a fish out of water as Frank Yallop's replacement, and the general manager Alexi Lalas both left. At one point they won one game in fifteen, and Beckham, whose few highlights included scoring into an empty net from his own half against Kansas City, did not make the MLS team of the season.

His popularity was not helped by joining Milan on loan from January 2009 and then extending his stay until mid-June. At his first match back, one supporter's banner famously read 'Go home fraud' and Beckham leapt over a barrier and confronted a particularly abusive fan – just, he insisted unconvincingly, to shake hands.

The experienced new coach, Bruce Arena, better at handling the whole circus than Yallop or Gullit had been, had targeted a total of 25 points by the time of the prodigal son's return in mid-season; the Galaxy managed 24 of them and after that as Arena said in his understated way, 'when David came, it obviously made us a little bit of a different team'.

By the end of the regular season the points total was up to 48, just enough to finish top of the Western Conference table, pipping Houston Dynamo (who had a better goal difference) on head-to-head results. In the play-offs, the Galaxy beat Chivas and then Houston to qualify for their first final since 2006, against Real Salt Lake – a club in only their fifth season of MLS.

A tight game was expected, four of the previous six meetings between the clubs having been finished level, including a 2-2 draw after three goals were scored in added time.

On the morning of the final, discussion centred around a familiar topic: 'David Beckham is nursing a bone bruise in his right foot.' Bruce Arena, preparing for his fourth MLS final, was promising 'David will be fine.' Reporters, aware that he had not been able to train for several days after the recent Conference final against Houston, appeared sceptical but should have known better.

'It's just one of those things you have to get through. After 5 or 10 minutes of the game I'm sure I'll forget about it,' he told them, while Landon Donovan, despite his occasional frustration with the Galaxy's other superstar, paid tribute to him: 'David's been hurt or sick for probably the last six or seven games but he gets on with it and he plays – that's helped our team a lot.'

Playing through the pain was nothing new and would be eased only a little by three pre-match injections; but the real hurt would come from defeat, by that most English of means - penalties.

LA Galaxy: Ricketts (Saunders, 66), Franklin, Berhalter, Gonzalez (DeLaGarza, 89), Dunivant, Donovan, Beckham, Birchall (Klein, 79), Magee, Buddle, Kirovski.
Real Salt Lake: Rimando, Olave, Borchers, Russell, Wingert, Morales (Mathis, 22), Beckerman, Williams, Johnson (Grabavoy, 46), Movsisyan (Espindola, 75), Findley.
Attendance: 46,011

For 20 minutes, the elusive first American championship seemed to be within Beckham's grasp, after he played his part in putting the Galaxy ahead shortly before half-time. Mike Magee had earlier wasted his side's best chance, shooting across goal from a good position, but he finished more accurately with a neat side-footed volley after Beckham had played in Donovan down the right for a perfect cross.

In the 64th minute, however, Beckham's determined tracking back, leaving him as the last defender, could not prevent the US international and former Galaxy striker Robbie Findley scoring an equaliser after a bout of pinball in the penalty area. Soon extra-time was beckoning. Beckham was not welcoming it on another artificial pitch and at the end of normal time he could be seen taking off his boot and rubbing his troublesome foot.

The extra half-an-hour brought no further goals, necessitating a shoot-out. Beckham stepped up for the first penalty and was for that brief moment grateful that a true surface lay beneath him, rather than one that would give way as in Istanbul or Lisbon. He sent the goalkeeper the wrong way to give his team the lead, quickly cancelled out by Clint Mathis.

Although Donovan of all people failed, shooting high over the bar, it was level at 4-4 after six kicks apiece. Then Galaxy's Edson Buddle had his attempt saved by Nick Rimando, and Salt Lake's Robbie Russell, born in Ghana and signed from Norwegian football, placed his kick just inside a post to win the cup.

At least the city of angels could be a little prouder of its team. 'It was a bitter end to a memorable season,' wrote the *LA Times* correspondent, adding, 'In a championship game that never rose to any great heights, spectacular plays were few and far between. But it was also a game that matched two teams of equal skill and determination.'

'It's Russian roulette,' said a disappointed Beckham, who was used to that by now. 'It's not a nice way to go but it's the way it is in soccer.' His time would come, but not for another two years.

47

Manchester United 4 AC Milan 0
(United won 7-2 on Aggregate)
Champions League knockout Round
(Old Trafford)
10 March 2010

Desperate to maintain his England place, Beckham returned to Europe from Los Angeles each January, first to train with Arsenal (2008), then to play for AC Milan (2009 and 2010), who were twice unable to prevent their co-tenants Inter winning *Serie A*. On his first stay at the San Siro there was only one round of European football to play, when the Italians went out of the UEFA Cup to eventual finalists Werder Bremen on away goals, but the following year brought the unexpected consequence of playing twice against Manchester United and then the unwanted one of an Achilles injury that would end his England career.

While he was reaching the MLS Cup Final (see previous chapter), the team of Andrea Pirlo, Clarence Seedorf, Thiago Silva and Ronaldinho did him a favour by qualifying for the knockout stage of the Champions League as group runners-up to Real Madrid. The draw, almost inevitably, pitted them against United, who since his departure seven years earlier had claimed three successive Premier League titles, three League Cups, one FA Cup (from three finals) and won the 2008 Champions League before losing the following year's final.

In an exciting first leg in Italy – 'the first time I've wanted Manchester United to lose' Beckham said beforehand – his old club were victorious 3-2 after falling behind; his free-kick led to the opening goal for Ronaldinho before he was substituted after 72 minutes, whereupon Wayne Rooney scored his second goal for a 3-1 lead. Then just before the finish Beckham's replacement Seedorf reduced the deficit and Michael Carrick was sent off.

United's manager was determined that his players should not be complacent ahead of the second leg, when *The Guardian's* preview was headlined 'Ferguson warns United are still on a tightrope as Beckham circus hits town'.

'Beckham being Beckham, he needed a police escort when he arrived at Manchester airport,' wrote Daniel Taylor, suggesting it would be one of those Champions League nights that counted as 'an occasion' more than just a match.

'I wanted to stay at Old Trafford for my whole career,' United's former hero had told the media rather wistfully before his one and only return there as an opposition player.

'But sometimes things aren't meant to be. It would have been great to stay like Ryan Giggs has.'

Ferguson correctly predicted he would be only a substitute on the night, but there was to be one final Old Trafford cameo.

Manchester United: Van der Sar, G. Neville (Rafael, 66), Ferdinand, Vidic, Evra, Valencia, Park, Fletcher, Scholes (Gibson, 73), Nani, Rooney (Berbatov, 66).
Milan: Abbiati, Abate (Beckham, 64), Bonera (Seedorf, 46), Thiago Silva, Jankulovski, Flamini, Pirlo, Ambrosini, Ronaldinho, Borriello (Inzaghi, 68), Huntelaar.
Attendance: 74,595.

As well as having Carrick suspended, United were also without the injured Giggs, Anderson and Owen Hargreaves, but they need not have worried. The match was straightforward enough, for an ageing Milan were unable to make a contest of it. As the *Daily Mail* wrote of them, 'This was as depressing an evening as this once great side have had in Europe for many a year. Further evidence that they have become sporting geriatrics.'

Rooney put them behind early on, heading in Gary Neville's excellent cross, and added his second goal of the night immediately after half-time from Nani's run and pass. That was the key moment, Ferguson said later, and when Park Ji-Sung drove in Paul Scholes' pass it was a good time for Beckham to appear, as a substitute for Ignazio Abate. The tie was decided; Old Trafford was in celebratory mood and he received the warmest of welcomes from all round the ground. 'Welcome home' and 'Thanks for everything Becks' the banners read.

The crowd would not have begrudged him a goal, which he almost managed with a vicious 20-yard volley that Edwin Van der Sar pushed over the bar. Milan's evening got even worse, however, when Darren Fletcher headed in Rafael's accurate long cross for the fourth goal. 'Not many teams have beaten Milan 4-0,' Ferguson pointed out.

The other subplot to the night was the ongoing protest by United supporters against the club's unpopular owners, the Glazer family, two of whom were present. Beckham appeared to have joined it by donning a yellow-and-green scarf as he waved his farewells after the game, only to offer a more mundane and diplomatic explanation later: 'I'm a Manchester United fan and when I saw the scarf I wanted to put it round my neck. It's the old colours of United but to be honest it's not my business. It's got nothing to do with me how it's run. I just support the team.'

In an interview with Sky Sports he said,

Obviously it's always disappointing when you lose games as important as this one but we've come up against a great United side tonight. The thing I'll take from it is the reception I got, which was unbelievable. It meant a lot. It's definitely up there as one of my best nights, apart from the results. It's a great club with a great manager and they deserve to go all the way.

To his further disappointment, that did not happen. United were a little unfortunate to be drawn in the quarter-final against Bayern Munich, who scored late goals against them in both legs to go through on away goals after winning 2-1 at home and losing 3-2 at Old Trafford.

Worse was the injury in Milan's very next game that put Beckham out of football until September; Britain's Poet Laureate, Carol Ann Duffy, was moved to write a poem entitled *Achilles*. On his return to MLS, the Galaxy finished top of the table for the second year running but were beaten in the Conference play-off final by Dallas. A national title would have to wait.

48

LA Galaxy 1 Houston Dynamo 0
MLS Final (Home Depot Center)
20 November 2011

Under the complicated MLS system, the two regional Conference league tables are merged together at the end of the season to provide an overall winner of the Supporters' Shield (and entrant to the Concacaf Champions League) before the play-offs. Progressing through the play-off matches to become actual MLS champions has historically proved difficult, with only five teams having done it in fifteen years before 2011.

As noted at the end of Chapter 47, the Galaxy suffered this familiar fate in 2010, having the best regular season record of any club but losing their Western Conference final 3-0 to Dallas (who were then beaten in the MLS final by Colorado Rapids). So although Houston's Glaswegian-born coach Dominic Kinnear had called David Beckham's side 'the best team in the league from day one', and the Home Depot Center had been chosen in May as the venue for the final, nobody in LA was taking anything for granted when they finished as Supporters' Shield winners for the second year running.

Allowing for the usual injury concerns (back problems and a torn hamstring), now accepted as a hazard of a thirty-six-year-old footballer's life, the season had gone more smoothly than any of Beckham's previous four – mainly, it could be argued, because instead of joining a European club on loan in the off-season he merely trained for a while with Tottenham.

From a defeat by Dallas at the start of May the Galaxy went on a long unbeaten league run extending fifteen games and three months. The only concern was that even with Beckham chipping in (or curling in) the occasional free-kick, they were not prolific scorers, managing only eleven goals in ten matches during one period of that successful spell. The solution was the arrival from Spurs in August, for a fee reported to be $4 million, of Robbie Keane, who settled in immediately with a goal on his debut at home to San Jose in front of a 27,000 Home Depot Center crowd.

The Galaxy duly finished 4 points ahead of Seattle Sounders, unbeaten in sixteen home games and achieving the second highest points total (67) in MLS history. In the play-offs they overcame the New York Red Bulls (3-1 on aggregate), and Real Salt Lake (3-1) to reach a second MLS final in three years.

Beckham's twenty-six appearances were more than in any of his previous seasons and he received an official award as the MLS 'Comeback Player of the year', his ten yellow cards taken as evidence of commitment and desire rather than indiscipline and slower reactions.

With Beckham's contract due to run out at the end of the season, there was naturally intense speculation that this could be his last competitive game. At a BBC dinner in the summer, old admirer Sven-Goran Eriksson, back in English football as manager of Leicester City, had sounded out David about signing, prompting Victoria's famous line, 'Sven, can you see me in Leicester?'

In July he had told British journalists covering the Galaxy's 1-1 draw with Manchester City that he expected to continue: 'One, maybe two more years. I'm still enjoying getting up in the morning to go training and, until that changes, I don't see any reason to stop just yet.' One new incentive was to play for Team GB in the London Olympics the following summer: 'I'd love to be involved and, for that to happen, I still have to be playing by then.'

The *LA Times* nevertheless pointed out, 'He has already raised MLS' profile, tripled the Galaxy's annual revenue and made the league a destination for other international stars,' adding that if the Galaxy were finally to win an MLS title for him, 'he would seem to be out of challenges here'.

Meanwhile the supporters' banner reading 'Go home fraud' was no longer in evidence, and those that were said 'Beckham stay here' and 'Beckham, LA loves you'. The feeling appeared to be mutual: a week before the final he recounted his almost childish excitement at spotting Al Pacino walking his dog.

LA Galaxy: Saunders, Franklin, Gonzalez, DeLaGarza, Dunivant, Donovan, Beckham, Juninho, Magee, Keane, Cristman.
Houston Dynamo: Hall, Hainault, Boswell, Cameron, Taylor, Cruz (Clark, 78), Camargo, Moffatt, Ashe (Watson, 84), Ching, Carr (Costly, 66).
Attendance: 30,281.

Given the confidence established over the whole season and the advantage of playing a 'home' game, the Galaxy dominated from the start and should have been ahead well before their opponents forced a clear chance. One player seemed to be behind most of those opportunities. As Tom Dart, an English reporter working in the US, put it in *The Times,*

Beckham raged with the same crazed determination as in the famous game against Greece, in which he single-handedly shoved England into the 2002 World Cup finals. Then, his performance was extraordinary because he was everywhere, a turbine in perpetual motion. On Sunday, after months of back problems and sabotaged by a torn hamstring, he could barely jog and certainly not run. Silken feet capped wooden legs. This was not an act of defiance against the opposition, against the danger of defeat – it was a magnificent resistance to a betrayal by his body.

Adam Cristman, Keane's partner in attack, was particularly wasteful, missing with a free header from a Beckham corner and then nodding wide again when Beckham put another cross on his head. Before half-time Keane, coming from right to left, played in the normally reliable Mike Magee, who shot far too high, but the pattern continued into the second half.

Twice Keane was sent through by Beckham: after clipping a shot across goal he put the second chance through the goalkeeper Tally Hall's legs, only to be given offside when replays proved he was level with the last defender.

A header from Glaswegian Adam Moffat, once of Elgin City, at the other end in the sixty-sixth minute from Corey Ashe's cross was a warning that the Galaxy heeded 6 minutes later. For once Beckham's contribution was a header, deftly flicked into Keane's path. The Irishman, only just keeping control on a soft, wet pitch, managed to come inside his man before releasing Landon Donovan to flick just inside the far post with the outside of his foot.

Beckham almost had the last word. A free-kick from well outside the penalty area somehow curved back and was dropping under the bar until Hall clawed it away. As Beckham jogged wearily over to take the corner and travelling Houston fans greeted him with a hail of paper cups, the referee grabbed the ball and concluded the final.

Coach Bruce Arena, aware of how debilitating his captain's injuries had been, said of him, 'I've been around great athletes and competitors in different sports. And this guy's as good as it gets. He gutted it out tonight'.

'I've wanted to be successful for the Galaxy for five years, and tonight I have,' Beckham said, having become the only Englishman other than Trevor Steven (Everton, Rangers and Marseille) to have won the championship in three countries.

Remarkably, he had a fourth to come. But all the reports linking him at the end of 2011 with the newly enriched Paris Saint-Germain would prove premature.

49

LA Galaxy 3 Houston Dynamo 1
MLS Final (Home Depot Center)
1 December 2012

Despite all the speculation linking him with Paris and elsewhere, David Beckham stayed in Los Angeles for another season – albeit one interrupted by his duties at the London Olympics. Not as a player, however: Great Britain's manager Stuart Pearce decided to select Ryan Giggs instead for the final over-age spot and the captaincy, leaving Beckham to star in the opening ceremony by racing up the River Thames in a speedboat carrying the Olympic flame.

By that time, at the end of July, the Galaxy were only just getting their season back on track, having won a mere three games from the first thirteen and been bottom of the table. Once Beckham was back and able to concentrate fully on the team, results had begun to improve, Landon Donovan suggesting, 'David's demeanour was influencing everybody. He declared at that point he was going to take control. And we all bought into it.'

At that stage Beckham had probably already decided he would be leaving at the end of the season, although the official announcement was not made until 20 November, just after the Galaxy reached a second successive MLS final by coming through the play-offs against Vancouver (2-1), San Jose (3-2 aggregate) and Seattle (4-2 aggregate). That clever marketing strategy naturally did no harm to levels of interest in the final, which would be watched in 157 countries.

The opposition, just like the previous year, would be Houston Dynamo and Beckham's club would again be playing in their home stadium. For the first time, whichever of the finalists had the better record over the regular season could stage the final. Although the Galaxy's was modest - having finished only fourth in the Western Conference with 54 points from thirty-four games – that was still 1 point better than Houston in the Eastern Conference.

The questionable new system guaranteed a big crowd but obviously offered one of the clubs a huge advantage. That club was the Galaxy again, and Houston were forced to take what belief they could from having won 1-0 at the Home Depot Center in a pre-season friendly (when all twenty outfield players were changed at half-time) and seen eight visiting teams emerge victorious during the MLS campaign from a ground where the Galaxy had been impregnable the previous year.

LA Galaxy: Saunders; Franklin, Gonzalez, Meyer, Dunivant, Wilhelmsson (Buddle, 74), Beckham (Sarvas, 89), Juninho (Stephens, 76), Magee, Donovan, Keane.
Houston Dynamo: Hall; Sarkodie (Ching, 77), Taylor, Boswell, Ashe, Garcia, Moffat (Barnes, 71), Clark, Davis, Bruin, Carr (Kandji, 59)
Attendance: 30,510.

It may have been 1,400 miles between the two cities, but the Dynamo still had a good representation of orange-clad supporters, and they were the ones celebrating a half-time lead.

That was only because Donovan, who had done nothing to quell speculation that he too might be leaving Los Angeles, had wasted a glorious chance after 12 minutes. Beckham's classic long pass found Robbie Keane running into space and with all the time he needed to square a pass for Donovan, who hit it wide from barely 8 yards. Beckham-Keane-Donovan: exactly the play that had won the cup a year earlier, but with an outcome this time that recalled one description of the American forward as 'mentally and physically exhausted'.

Mike Magee, like Keane and Donovan a scorer of crucial goals in the play-offs, then headed a Beckham free-kick down into the ground and wide from even closer in. Houston threatened through Brad Davis and right-back Kofi Sarkodie before going ahead just a minute before the interval. Calen Carr, just onside, broke onto a pass in the inside-right channel from Adam Moffat and ran on to beat Josh Saunders.

The second half was a different tale and it was hardly a surprise that Beckham's right foot should have a part to play. Early on his free-kick led to Keane beating the goalkeeper Tally Hall, only to be given offside. Then an inswinging Beckham corner forced Hall to punch out under pressure and before Houston cleared, 6ft-5in defender Omar Gonzalez headed in Juninho's cross. It was a triumphant moment for a player who had missed the first four months of the campaign with a serious knee injury.

An hour had been played and within a few more minutes the Galaxy had a goal disallowed and scored again. After the referee wrongly penalised Gonzalez for pushing as he set up Keane to score, Ricardo Clark handled Keane's shot and Donovan composed himself sufficiently to convert the penalty.

One breakaway and shot driven wide by Houston's Brian Ching was the only nervous moment for the home majority, who had another goal to celebrate before the final whistle. In added time Hall was ruled to have fouled Keane as the Irishman dribbled past him and although sentimentality might have demanded that Beckham take the kick, Keane himself planted it past the goalkeeper.

Coach Bruce Arena, demonstrating a greater sense of showmanship than the striker, immediately substituted Beckham, allowing him a farewell all of his own to a crowd who seemed to have forgiven the 'fraud' of three years earlier.

A delighted Arena said later,

Twenty years from now, we are going to look at this league and still talk about David Beckham as the one that helped turn us. For him to walk off the field today with another trophy is amazing. Many would think it was the last chapter. I think David thinks there is another chapter, and if there is, it's probably going to be a great chapter.

Ian Ladyman, Manchester-based reporter for the *Daily Mail,* wrote,

As a football technician, he remains almost unparalleled. Here today, some of his passing was reminiscent of his salad days at Manchester United and Real Madrid. Playing deep in the centre of midfield, the 37-year-old found the time and space to deliver telling passes with familiar regularity.

The thirty-seven-year-old in question, meanwhile, claimed to have no knowledge of where he would be playing next, only that he did not want to retire prematurely like his friend Paul Scholes, who had recently had to ask Manchester United to take him back:

I do know that I am happy to have been part of this club for six years and been successful for the last four years. I will continue with my commitment to this league. I might not be playing here anymore but my commitment to growing this sport and this league will continue. I plan to keep playing as long as I can, as long as my legs will take me.

Just as there are varied opinions about most things to do with Beckham, so his effect on football in the US was no different. During his five years there gates rose by 20 per cent, merchandise sales by 200 per cent and profile by an unquantifiable amount. Unquestionably, his time there encouraged some big names who could easily have stayed in Europe such as Thierry Henry, Kaka, Robbie Keane, Steven Gerrard and Frank Lampard to make the switch.

Ivan Gazidis, heavily involved in his recruitment to MLS, probably has it about right when he says, 'I don't think it was a critical signing for us, I think the League would have continued on a very positive trajectory, but it gave us a very nice impetus'.

Journalist Grant Wahl, borrowing from the title of his own 2009 book in offering a verdict three years later suggested:

In the end, I think the Beckham Experiment was worth it. Beckham brought more credibility to MLS the day he signed with Los Angeles, and he didn't treat his time here as a vacation. It didn't always go smoothly ... but he showed that his time here was a success on the field and not just from a business perspective.

50

Paris Saint-Germain 3 Brest 1
Ligue 1 (Parc des Princes)
18 May 2013

'The next move will be a move that is about the football,' Beckham said on his departure from Los Angeles, quickly adding, lest there should be any misunderstanding about the past five years, 'That has never been any different for me. I just want to play for the best team and with the best players.'

His representatives held on until the last day of the January 2013 transfer window, when it became clear that Paris Saint-Germain would be the next and final destination. French club football may have lagged behind Spain, Germany, England and Italy but in PSG there seemed to be an emerging force, one that the country's capital city lacked until a Qatari takeover in 2011 provided the necessary financial support.

Beckham had almost moved there at the end of that year, having finally won an MLS title, but family and lifestyle considerations prompted him to stay in LA for another twelve months. By that point, time was clearly running out if the 'last challenge' was to be undertaken anywhere near the top level of European football. Fortunately PSG's Carlo Ancelotti, previously his coach at Milan, was still keen to have him; and he would be joining a team top of the table and in the last sixteen of the Champions League.

Runners-up to Montpellier the previous season, PSG spent more than £100 million in the summer on players of the quality of Zlatan Ibrahimovic, Ezequiel Lavezzi, Thiago Silva and Marco Verratti, all from Italian clubs, plus the teenage Brazilian midfielder Lucas Moura, who was loaned back to Sao Paulo until January. That sort of ambition, naked as it was, impressed Beckham, who explained that he 'chose Paris because I can see what the club are trying to do, I can see the players the club are bringing in. It's an exciting city and always has been but now there's a club that will have a lot of success over the next ten, fifteen and twenty years.'

After starting the season unpromisingly with three draws, two of them at home, they had quickly improved, hitting the top of the table after nine games before briefly dropping to fourth early in December.

Back on top by the winter transfer window, they still exercised the option to bring in Lucas Moura, who had cost 40 million euros. Money was clearly no great object, even with the introduction of Uefa's Financial Fair Play legislation, and whether or not Beckham was embarrassed by the size of his salary, he decided to give all of it during his five-month stay (estimated at £3.5 million) to local children's charities – a decision greeted with more cynicism in some quarters than it deserved. There was further criticism when it did not immediately happen, but matters were eventually sorted out with the tax authorities.

His debut did not come until 24 February as a late substitute in the 2-0 home win against great rivals Olympique Marseille, in between the two legs of the Champions League knockout round, in which (without him) PSG beat Valencia 3-2 on aggregate. Beckham's final contribution in that tournament was to play in both legs of the quarter-final against Barcelona, where his new team went out despite two creditable draws – 2-2 at home and 1-1 away.

Booked in the second leg, he also suffered the ignominy of a red card late in the away game at Evian, but was back as a (very) late substitute on the day PSG secured the league title for only the third time in their forty-year history, and first since 1994, with a 1-0 victory at Lyon. Modest as his contribution may have been, it was, of course, Beckham's fourth in different countries.

On 16 May his retirement was officially announced, to take place at the end of the season a week later, meaning that the home game against Brest would be his last at the Parc des Princes. Although there was still one further *Ligue 1* match to play, away to Lorient (the English club Leyton Orient actually had to field calls asking if it was against them), it became clear that he would not be involved there. Saturday 18 May in Paris really would be the last goodbye; coincidentally, one day before Sir Alex Ferguson's final match in charge of Manchester United.

Paris Saint-Germain: Sirigu (Areola, 48), Sakho, Tiene, Camara, Jallet, Matuidi, Chantome (Moura, 46), Pastore, Beckham (Lavezzi, 82), Ibrahimovic, Gameiro.
Brest: Thebaux, Makonda, Sissoko, Licka, Dieng (Chardonnet, 63), Grougi, Soumah, Ba (Benschop, 78), Lesoimier, Chafni, Raspentino (Khaled, 72).
Attendance: 44,983.

The Beckham clan, including parents, wife and four children, (in addition to celebrities like the former French president Nicolas Sarkozy), were all at the stadium to see him lead PSG out after being made captain for the night. It may have been only his fifth start for the team, but the crowd were aware of being present on a special occasion and roared their approval when his name was read out.

If Carlo Ancelotti feared an anticlimax, especially when bottom-of-the-table Brest started the game brightly, worries were quickly assuaged. In the sixth minute Beckham started a move that led to Ibrahimovic veering past his marker to score with an angled drive, earning a kiss from the captain. A few minutes later Beckham's 50-yard pass gave the Swede another chance, denied him by the goalkeeper Alexis Thebaux, but just after the half-hour there was a genuine Beckham set-piece assist, a corner from which Blaise Matuidi scored the second goal.

A third followed before half-time, when Ibrahimovic exercised his rights to take free-kicks and beat Thebaux with a beauty from 25 yards. He almost completed a hat-trick before the interval, putting a half-volley wide.

If the second half proved to be less eventful, the crowd did not appear to mind, even when the Dutch striker Charlison Benschop scored for the visitors with 9 minutes left. By that time Beckham appeared physically and emotionally exhausted and Lavezzi was waiting on the touchline to replace him. He departed in tears to a touching ovation, and hugs all round from teammates, then Ancelotti and English coach Paul Clement, plus most of the players in the dug-outs from both clubs.

After 834 games, with 146 goals, and too many assists to count, it really was all over. Tributes came from, among many others, the FA chairman David Bernstein ('As an ambassador for the English game I could not think of anyone better') and even the Prime Minister David Cameron's spokesman: ('An outstanding footballer and a brilliant ambassador for his country'.)

One or two critics, notably in *The Independent,* quibbled that he was 'finished as a footballer long ago' and was 'never a great player', while still admitting 'none trained harder or was better prepared'.

Martin Samuel in the *Daily Mail* was more generous, suggesting, 'For a man who was only picked to sell shirts, it turned out quite a career.' And the lyrical Simon Barnes offered this summing up in *The Times*: 'At the heart of Beckham-mania was Beckham the footballer. Beckham's was a career full of meaning and incident. It was a great story – and he was so nearly a great footballer.'

Last word to the man himself, who told Sky Sports, 'I just want people to see me as a hard-working footballer. Someone that is passionate about the game. People have obviously looked at certain other things throughout my career and I think sometimes that's overshadowed what I've done on the pitch and achieved on the pitch. I was fortunate to have realised dreams.'

Acknowledgments

Many thanks to Steve McClaren for the foreword, Cliff Butler at Manchester United for statistical detail and Grant Cameron of BBC Sport Northern Ireland for assistance with Chapter 1, plus Ivan Gazidis, Robert Lee, Danny Mills, Phil Shaw, Nick Szczepanik and Joan Walley MP.

Extracts from *My Side* by David Beckham reprinted by permission Harper Collins Publishers Ltd. Copyright © Footwork Productions Ltd, 2003.

Extracts from *David Beckham My Son* by Ted Beckham by permission of Macmillan. Copyright Ted Beckham, 2005.

Extract from *White Angels* by John Carlin by permission of Bloomsbury Publishing Plc. © John Carlin, 2004.

From *Managing My Life* by Alex Ferguson and *After The Ball* by Nobby Stiles by permission of Hodder and Stoughton Ltd. © 1999 Alex Ferguson and 2003 Nobby Stiles.

From *My Life, My Story* by Ryan Giggs by permission of Headline Publishing Group. © 2010 Ryan Giggs Limited.

From *My 1998 World Cup Story* by Glenn Hoddle by permission of Carlton Publishing Group.

From *Red: My Autobiography* by Gary Neville (2011), published by Bantam Press, by permission of The Random House Group Ltd.

Bibliography & Sources

Adams, Tony *Addicted* (Collins Willow, 2008)

Astaire, Simon *Sol Campbell* (Spellbinding Media, 2014)

Auclair, Philippe *Cantona* (Macmillan, 2009)

Beckham, David *My World* (Hodder & Stoughton, 2001)

Beckham, David *David Beckham* (Headline, 2013)

Crick, Michael *The Boss* ((Simon & Schuster, 2002)

Davies, David *FA Confidential* (Simon & Schuster, 2008)

Eriksson, Sven-Goran *My Story* (Headline, 2013)

Ferguson, Alex *My Autobigraphy* (Hodder & Stoughton, 2014)

Joseph, Paul *Thierry Henry, Fifty Defining Fixtures* (Amberley, 2014)

Keane, Roy *The Autobiography* (Michael Joseph, 2002)

Keane, Roy *The Second Half* (Weidenfeld & Nicolson, 2014)

Lovejoy, Joe *Sven* (Collins Willow, 2002)

McCartney, Iain *Sir Alex Ferguson, Fifty Defining Fixtures* (Amberley, 2013)

McManaman, Steve *El Macca* ((Simon & Schuster, 2002)

Marcotti, Gabriele *Capello* (Bantam Press, 2008)

Meek, David and Tyrell, Tom *Manchester United In Europe* (Coronet, 2002)

Owen, Michael *Off the Record* (Collins Willow, 2004)

Palmer, Myles *The Professor* (Virgin, 2001)

Russell, Gwen *Arise Sir David Beckham* (John Blake, 2008)

Wahl, Grant *The Beckham Experiment* (Crown Books, USA, 2009)

Yousif, Layth *Arsene Wenger, Fifty Defining Fixtures* (Amberley, 2014)

Rothmans Football Yearbook, (Headline 1992–2001)

Sky Sports Football Yearbook (Headline, 2002–2013)

National newspapers and their websites, plus www.soccerbase.co.uk

L'Equipe, Los Angeles Times, New York Times, Washington Post.

About the Author

Steve Tongue, who has been a sports journalist and broadcaster for forty-five years, watched David Beckham's first match for Manchester United in 1992 and has followed his career with particular interest ever since. He tweets @stevetongue.